T0304592

THE BRONX STREET KID BECOMES A MAN

THE BRONX STREET KID BECOMES A MAN

RICHARD KANE

authorHOUSE®

AuthorHouse™
1663 Liberty Drive
Bloomington, IN 47403
www.authorhouse.com
Phone: 1-800-839-8640

© *2013 by Richard Kane. All rights reserved.*

No part of this book may be reproduced, stored in a retrieval system, or transmitted by any means without the written permission of the author.

Published by AuthorHouse   12/20/2012

ISBN: 978-1-4772-9795-7 (sc)
ISBN: 978-1-4772-9796-4 (e)

Any people depicted in stock imagery provided by Thinkstock are models, and such images are being used for illustrative purposes only.
Certain stock imagery © Thinkstock.

This book is printed on acid-free paper.

Because of the dynamic nature of the Internet, any web addresses or links contained in this book may have changed since publication and may no longer be valid. The views expressed in this work are solely those of the author and do not necessarily reflect the views of the publisher, and the publisher hereby disclaims any responsibility for them.

DECEMBER 1
THE BRONX STREET KID BECOMES A MAN
Richard Kane
Sober date June 20, 2001

DECEMBER 2011

My journey continues as I grow up, I am learning to become a man. The 12 steps are the way to achieve a God realized life. When I let go, I let God. He is the king of the universe and he provides all my needs. When I have a problem that confuses me. I can say I may not know how to find a spiritual solution however, I do recognize that a spiritual solution exists. There is a force in the universe that has all power and all answers. I ask for a miracle, I am asking that something inside of me change. As I get softer, I find inner peace. When I remove the fear that blocks love. I become Gods instrument. I become a miracle worker, and when I say I am on the earth to serve GOD. That means I am on the earth to love. I have a mission to help save the world. With the power of love. When I choose to be a teacher of GODS mission. I must be loving and forgiven. Angry people cannot create a peaceful world. My practice of forgiveness is very important and a contribution to the healing of the world. When I surrender my past, to the Holy Spirit. I ask that only loving helpful thoughts remain and that all the rest I let go. I am then left with the present. The only time where miracles happen. When I plug into God, I plug into the spiritual infinite force I immediately let go of fear, judgment, and negativity.

DECEMBER1, 2011

When my life is over were will I go. I am going to heaven. I have wandered around in my small little world. My accomplishments will not amount to anything, 5-minutes after I am dead, my stuff will end up in a dumpster. The only thing worthwhile in my life is my Sobriety and helping others. Love is what I am here to teach and learn. When I let go of fear and hatred. I find love. God is love. Where love is God is. The 12step recovery meetings offer me a chance to Love and do service. One drunk helping another that is pure human love at its finest. I also realize when I hurt another human being I am also hurting myself. I must learn to use the law of attraction in a healthier way. My old life has to be ripped out, and replaced with pure thinking. The 7th step prayer is about getting the impure thoughts and actions out of my life. This is a painful process because I am becoming more aware of them these are the blocks that must be removed the ego has to smashed and then replaced with good thoughts from God.

DECEMBER 2011

Freddy king sings the darkest hour is just a little bit before the dawn. This is true I have come to realize and know that my personal history all exists in my mind. The present moment is all I have. I just find it very hard to stay in the moment all the time. When I heard about the sex abuse at Penn state, of course I am a victim of that crime. I started to feel some of my pain. Anyway, it's not real anymore after all the abuse stopped a long time ago. Some people told me to stop playing victim. I realize these people didn't get raped at age 7 so they don't know the emotional pain I stuffed and suffered with for over 40years. I personally don't think I get over something like that. I think I go through the pain accepting what was done and feel my feelings and then let them go. Because of this I am getting better. I have the spirit of the universe living inside of me. That power will guide me too where I gotta be to get better. Love is the answer. Forgiveness is part of love. I have hope and a dream. GOD is pure love and my provider.

DECEMBER 2011

Jesus said give up resisting an evil person. Resist no evil means I give up fighting my problems. When I become a fighter against anything. I join forces with that which created the problem. I react with a counterforce. When Mother Teresa was asked during the Vietnam War, will you join our march against the war? She said no, but if you have a march for peace, I will be there. Fighting against war is just another war. This same logic applies to worldwide conflicts, like Northern Ireland and the Middle East. When we put our collective energy on what we are for, bringing kindness and love to our differences. We can end the illusion of hatred, anger and repression. It is only through a change in consciousness, that our world will be transformed. This is true in my life and all problems as well. Here is something I heard. The masters of life know the way they listen to the voice within, the voice of wisdom and simplicity, the voice that reasons beyond cleverness and knows beyond knowledge. That voice is not just the power and property of a few, but has been given to everyone. It is the key to harnessing the power of the uncarved block. This law applies to my own dark side to fight my demons or to be angry with myself for the errors of my ways. I can say I believed in the delusion that I was separate from God, and I acted on that. Now I will bring the one power of Good to these thoughts of anguish and they will be nullified. The very presence of light takes away all darkness. I send love to my dark side and watch it dissolve and raise my spiritual energy.

DECEMBER 2011

I have the ability to change. God makes that possible. I have to understand that certain events from my past had a big impact on me. A part of me is the wounded child. I also have the sacred inner child,

I must continue to grow and listen to the sacred inner voice. That is the place were God lives in me. With Gods help and guidance, I can overcome everything I depend on God and the healing power of love. God has forgiven and forgot everything. I must do the same. God wants me to overcome the obstacles from my past. There are many of them. One day at a time, I allow God to help me forget the pain there is a lot of confusion that lives inside of me. Although I act cocky, I am not sure of who I am. I forget that I am a grown man. I react like a 7-year-old abuse victim. My thinking is distorted I have many fears, and I feel like a failure, this is part of my dark side. At other times, I feel blessed. And I realize I am a child of the king of the universe. That all the stain from the abuse has been removed. I forget to remember this at certain times and slide back into old thinking. I ask God to purify my mind to cleanse my thoughts. I want my thoughts to be pure and hopeful i do not want to be stuck in the past I will let go of the fear I can change my mindset to positive. I must get rid of the excuse that this is to hard. I can be happy at all times THE answers are in the Bible and the big book also the 12and12. I take responsibility for my journey. The best definition for happiness is peace, tranquility, and serenity.

DECEMBER 2011

Jesus said pray for your enemies. The poet Longfellow said if we could read the secret history of our enemies we shall find in each mans sorrows and suffering enough to disarm all hostility. I realize the horror Hitler caused by the holocaust and the suffering of the millions that died. Isn't abortion the same thing? Look at all the lives that were never lived. A spiritual solution could be that we adopt the babies. We must cherish life. I have prayed for my enemies. When my heart becomes pure. I will look at them as my greatest teachers. Because they have allowed me to examine the emotions of anger and revenge, and then transcend them. I have been disappointed and hurt violently by many people. I send love to them all. The Buddha said we live happily indeed, not hating those who hate us. Why should I fear evil—When the one true power of GOD is here for me. Simply put God is love and all he made is made in love. The actions and thoughts that I think are evil. Is the result of people thinking they are separate from God. The power of one is the power of love. God does not condemn, God forgives. God does not punish God is love. I accept and I am responsible for my mind. Because I can change my thoughts and attitudes. I have to train my mind to pause think and then act, as I think the higher power would want me to.

DECEMBER 2011

When I ask God to heal my life, he shines a bright light on everything I end up seeing a lot of things maybe I rather not see. I have a lot of armor; I think it protects my heart. I must face my demons and the ugliness. It often seems that my life gets worse when I began to work deeply on myself I am starting to see the truth about the games I played. I thought I needed to distance myself through denial and disassociation this process is very painful and I am tempted to go backwards, as I have often done in the past. It takes courage to go forward—this is often called the path of the spiritual warrior. I must endure the sharp pains of self-discovery rather than taking the easy way out by numbing out the pain with alcohol. This is not easy I have to look the ego straight in the eye. Before I have the power to get rid of it. With Gods grace, I can outgrow the patterns of my ego. I take the good with the bad. The more I learn about the light within. The easier it is to forgive for not being perfect. I must remember my neuroses are my wounds I am afraid to look at them because I think I am bad. I think that if people saw the real me, they would recoil in horror. When I begin to see the truth, the light dazzles me. A course in miracles states I must face this ring of fear I have to slay the dragons. These dragons are my demons, my wounds; my ego is the way I deny love to others and myself. My ego and its patterns have to be rooted out and de toxed from my system, before the pure love within can have a chance to come out. If I am convinced, I am not good enough I will have a hard time accepting someone into my life who thinks I am. The only way I can accept some one finding me wonderful is if I think I am when I accept that I am wonderful this is death to the ego. When I discover the divinity within. I then have the ability to remove the illusions of illness, scarcity and evil this is harmony. And it creates a relationship with the spirit. This is my natural state of being this is who I am. In the Bible, it states my son you are always with me, and everything I have is yours. With God, all things are possible when I think something is missing from my life with out exception it stems from my failure to understand and apply Gods law of abundance and true love.—

DECEMBER 2011

I went on a men's retreat this weekend in Mahwah, New Jersey. I go once a year. Its helps me in my recovery and I do a yearly inventory of my life. I had another spiritual experience. I went for a walk up the mountain to the ski slope. We do it every year. I read a letter to God. I asked for a healing in my mind and emotions Because of my childhood I have a lot of inner turmoil and confusion. I felt good after I prayed and meditated on the mountain. I went and talked to Father Ken he is sober 38years. I told him my story and I talked to him about the stuff that still bothered me from my life Mostly it was still the abuse issues from my past. This priest been all over the world he even hung out with Mother Teresa. He has a gift for healing someone told him he is a favored son with God. He listened to my story and my pain I asked for him to bless me he touched me we hugged I felt a release. I have a new level of peace. It was nighttime I went out for a walk. I was looking at the moon and the stars. I saw this one star. It was the brightest star I ever seen in my whole life. I felt like this star was talking to me I felt the presence of the lord and I heard in my mind that I would be all right my mind is healed I have such peace the last 3 days. God keeps his promises.

DECEMBER 2011
TWO OF MY FAVORITE PRAYERS
"THE BALLPLAYERS PRAYER"

Dear GOD help me be a good player in this game of life. I don't ask for an easy place in the lineup. Put me anywhere you need me. I only ask that I can give you 100 percent of all I have. If all the hard line drives, seem to come my way. I thank you for the compliment. Help me to remember that you never send a player more trouble than he can handle, Help me O LORD to accept the bad break as part of the game. May I always play on the square no matter what others do. Help me to study the book so I will know the rules. Finally, God if the natural turn of events goes against me and I am benched for sickness or old age. Please help me to accept that as part of the game too. Keep me from whimpering or squealing that I was framed or got a raw deal. When I finish the final inning I ask for no laurels. All I want is to believe in my heart that I played as well as I could and that I didn't let you down—AMEN

"A PRAYER TO LIVE WITH GRACE"

May we discover through pain and torment, the strength to live with grace and humor—may we discover through doubt and anguish the strength to live with dignity and holiness. May we discover through suffering and fear the strength to move toward healing. May it come to pass that we be restored to health and to vigor. May life grant us wellness of body, spirit, and mind. And if this cannot be so may we find in this transformation and passage moments of meaning, opportunities for love and the deep and gracious calm that comes when we allow ourselves to move on.

DECEMBER-8

Proverbs says for as a person thinks in his heart so is he. My actions are a direct result of my thoughts. If I have a negative mind, I will have a negative life. On the other hand when my mind is renewed by the word of God. Then my future is greater than my pastBecause ofGods grace he has put my past in the bottom of the sea and forgot it all. God puts a sign up—no fishing allowed here. I need a vision so I don't go back to my past. I gotta make my dreams bigger than my past. I gotta believe with God my dreams can come true. You know Rocky Graziano said somebody up there likes me. I here you brother, I know he likes me to. I believe something good is going to happen in my life today. God works through people. That is why 12 step groups are so effective. We need each other to stay sober. I need to throw my excuzes out and say I can do what I gotta do. God is positive not negative. I can have joy in my life. I gotta work at being posistive. Because of my past I am so used to being negative. I can over come all of this. I gotta believe there is good in everything. And I will see Gods goodness while I am living here on earth right here and right now. I have lived by Murphys law I can reverse this, by believing that anything good can happen for me. I gotta develop the mindset—to stop complaining. I also have to develop the mindset that I obey God promptly. And then I do it

DECEMBER-2011 THE PATH OF THE SPIRITUAL WARRIOR

My approach toward fellow human beings should be like this Hindu—vow. The flies seek filth, the bees seek honey. I will shun the habit of the flies and follow that of the Bee. I will refrain from finding fault in others, and look only for the good which is in them. This is something I should try to live up to. When I am on the path to becoming a spiritual warrior. I realize non attachment is self mastery—it is freedom from desire for what is seen or heard. I am on this path. And although I havent reached this stage of self mastery I am starting to realize that I can. Singleness of purpose is vital in my life, and so is unity. In 12 step groups we walk a spiritual path. With the goal of staying sober and helping another do the same. Perseverance is very important in this connection. No temporary failure, however disgraceful or humilating should ever be used as a excuze for giving up the struggle. No failure is ever really a failure unless we stop trying altogether. Indeed it may be a blessing in disguise and a much needed lesson. This lesson is true in my own life. When I went out and got drunk again after not drinking for over 12 years. I came back to the meetings. And simply did all the things I didn't do the other time. I got a sponsor, read the book and I did the step work I changed. As I make progress I am increasing in self mastery. I start to see I am renouncing nothing I really needed or wanted. I am freeing myself. In this spirit my soul grows in greatness. And then I can accept lifes worst disasters calm and unmoved. Christ said for my yoke is easy and my burden is light. A disciplined mind will set me free. I learn discipline by the practice of the12 steps I live in steps 10,11, and12-I do a daily meditation. I ask God to empower me and keep my mind free from dishonesty, resentment, and fear. The 11 steps puts me in right standing withGod the source of all power and strenght.

DECEMBER-2011

Until I have found God in my own soul, the whole world will seem meaningless. When I get up in the morning, I say this prayer. Dear God thank you for this day. Help me to stay clean and sober. Help me to recognize your hand in all things. Thank you for the blessings. I understand and the ones I don't. Thank you for your spirit who always abides in me. I ask that I may be with your spirit today. Cleanse my mind of all darkness and fill it with love and light. Let me be o.k-with this day no matter what it brings. Thank you for everything that's in life, and everything that's not. If I want to have a effective prayer life, and develop a good personal relationship with GOD. And know that he loves me. That he is full of mercy, that he will help me get to know Jesus who is my friend, and he died for me. I gotta get to know the holy spirit. The spirit is with me all the time and he wants to help me I gotta let him do that. And if I continue to studyGods word, I will know the truth, and acting on the truth will set me free. I must face the truth about my past, as God reveals it to me. My past may explain why I am suffering. I must not use it as a excuze to stay in bondage. I am without excuze because Jesus is ready to fufill his promise to set the captives free. JC will walk with me across the finish line to victory, if I am willing to go all the way with him.

DECEMBER-9-2011

I continue in my journey, I have learned to slow down my thoughts. I am a child of GOD. I must learn to be childlike, sometimes I am still childish. Like when I don't get my way. There is a lesson in this. I can choose peace. How can I look at these events differently. What is it about this, that I need to learn. Why do I get upset? Can this be solved, is there a solution. Yes there is. God has all power and every answer. God doesn't withhold anything. God is a giver, and he will give me all I need. Providing it is for the highest good and it doesn't hurt another person. God wants to be the director of my life, I have to invite GOD into my life, he is so kind that he will not interfere. When I get into trouble I call out toGod and ask him to help me. JC always comes through. No matter how much I screw up, he is there to clean me up. Because God is love, that is why he does that. Do you remember Dick Clark from american bandstand he was called the worlds oldest teenager. Anyway I am the worlds oldest juvenile deliguent. God has to watch over me all the time and he knows I need extra help. He sends guardian Angels like Rapheal and Micheal to protect and watch over me they gently guide me. Anything God asks me to do, I can do it. I can learn how to think right, The power of God is in me. And I am in right standing withGod. And I will not bow down to fear. I need to renew my mind and keep it renewed. Even when I am afraid I will do whatGod tells me and I must press through and finish what I started. I am determined to do whatGod called me to do. I must go forward with JC. The Red Sea didn't part until they put there foot in it. I have strenght to do all things through JC who strenghtens me. It is never to late to begin again and I will finish what I started I can have the victory because of the blood that JC spilled for me I am washed clean.

DECEMBER10-2011

They heat silver to get out the impurities. I am being purified byGod. I am being made Aware of my impure thinking which leads to my impure actions. They still exist in my life even though I am not drinking. I must become pure by allowing God to removethe impurities from life. Such as looking for pleasure in sex and watching and living in a fantasy world with porn. These behaviors are part of the sympton they stem from the root of selfishness and fear. All fear based behavior is from my ego—the shame, disgrace and dishonor all stem from my ego. From disgrace to grace is the answer. There is a purpose to my life. I must live my life for a higher purpose. I can have peace, love, and harmony also abundance of health and sobriety. As they say in 12 step recovery I gotta give it all away, so I can keep it. Because this is how I learn to be unselfish. I am here to serveGod. Because of the service work I do at 12 step meeting I am allowed the priviledge to be a servant. I carry the message of sobriety, hope, forgiveness and love. Through out history, God has used some strange broken people to do his work. Look at moses, he was a murderer yet he brought theJews out of Egypt. Look at King David and his family they were all messed up. God can take a messed up life and make a message out of it. He took me from brokeness to wholeness. I let love replace fear. I must awaken from the belief in 2 powers, good and evil. I begin to honor God by respecting the first commandment. The simple truth is that by thinking good healing loveing thoughts I can produce them. And by thinking evil thoughts I will produce that. I commit my life to the sustaining power ofGod the father once I do this, I stop fighting evil thoughts and instead embrace the oneness ofGOD. Divine love will meet every human need. Divine love is what I radiate outward. And it is not what ithink of as human love. In divine love there are no conditions. Divine love is a spiritual love and I must let divine love pour out from me.

DECEMBER-2011

The renewing of my mind will take place little by little. I must not get discouraged, when progress is slow. My pride is the beast that will consume me. If I receive too much freedom too quickly, my pride might think I am doing it. Its better I receive my freedom slowly in one area at a time. That way I will appreciate it more. I realize it is truly a gift from God and I cant do it on my own. Because of my drinking and my outlaw lifestyle I suffered. I needed to suffer so I could say that I have a problem. When JC-and12 step recovery delivered me from that pit, I rejoiced at my freedom and I said I am free free at last, and my heart overflows with thanksgiveing and praise. As GOD rises up and does for me what I couldn't do for myself I hit my knees and I say thank you. I will not condemn myself when I have setbacks or bad days. I just get back up, dust myself off, and start again. I have to accept the fact that along with my strenghts I also have weaknesses. I just let JC be strong in my weaknesses. I let him be my strenght on my weak days. The Bible repeatedly says do not be discouraged or dismayed, God knows that I will not come through to victory if I get discouraged. Also if I think condemning thoughts I am condemning myself. When I change my thinking I am set free. I start thinking like this—well things are going a little slow, but thank God I am making some progress. I am on the right path and I will be lead to freedom. Even though I make mistakes I can say that is one mistake I wont have to make again. This is a new day I will walk in the sunlight of the spirit. Today will be a great day. Jc you help me choose right thoughts. I must remember GOD is delivering me little by little. And I don't get discouraged or condemn myself when I make a mistake. I remember the Lord has begun a good work in me, and he will complete what he has started I must wait patiently on theLORD.

DECEMBER-2011

When I am connected to the spirit, I am not looking for occasions to be offended. And I am not judging or labeling others. I am then in a state of Grace. I know I am connected to God. My only problem is when I think I am separate fromGod. All my negative thoughts and feelings dissapear when I reconnect to God. All good comes from God and when I believe that all problems go away. my problems exist in my mind they are illusions. My condition is so strong that I have greater faith in my problems than I do in my ability to access a higher power and no longer have them. God gave his best for me. He paid the price he gave his son for my life. Am I giving my best to him-I have been washed clean by JC I am whiter than snow, the stain of my old life is forgiven and forgotten. I must be a instrument for God when I forgive I bring peace and my job is to extend love.

DECEMBER-2011

DON'T GIVE UP-No matter how bad the conditions in my life may be, I must not give up. In Galations the Apostle Paul encourages us to keep on keeping on, don't be a quitter. God is looking for people who will go all the way with him. Its easy to quit, it takes faith to go through to the end. The way God helps me is to strenghten and encourage me to keep going forward. When I begin to feel that this is to difficult and I am not going to make it. I have to cast down that kind of thinking—and choose to think that I am going to make it. Because of doubt and fear, I must take a stand and say I will never give up, God is on my side, he loves me and he is helping me. My thoughts become my words its vitally important that I choose good life generating thoughts. My mind is like a computer that has had a lifetime of garbage put into it. GOD is the best computer programer around I let God reprogram me, I also have invited JC to take control of my thoughts and I must keep cooperating with him. I had to realize iwas going nowhere with my life. I had many wrong mindsets I had been living of life of deception. There were a lot of strongholds. The LORD said you have dwelt long enough on this mountain. MY mountain was my childhood and the sex abuse I had been on that mountain over45years. I had to make a quality decision that I am going to get my mind renewed, and learn to choose my thoughts carefully. I must make up my mind that I will not quit or give up until victory is complete. And I have taken possesionof my rightful inheritanceI am a son ofGod and God wants me to be sober, happy, and free.

DECEMBER-3-2011

Gods love will overide all negative results from past abuse. There are two kinds of pain a abused person must face. The pain of change, or the pain of staying the same. Running from the past, does not lead to healing. I need to let go of the past and receive a inner strenghting, from God that will enable me to trust others and maintainhealthy intimate relationships and enjoy my life. God is a rewarder of those who seek him. I can learn to shake of trouble, and receive a double recompense for all I been through. Because of the trauma of abuse I couldn't function normally in everyday life. I had to learn how to gain victory over trauma. I am to seek the kingdom ofGOD which is within. My inner life with God is more important than my outer life. JC came to heal those who are broken inside. My wounded emotions became a prison, that locked me in and kept others out. I heal through noticing and prayer. Awareness alone does not heal, if analyis could heal my wounds I would be healed by now. The process of miraculous changeis twofold I see my error. I ask God to take it from me. As they say in AA, your best thinking got you here you're the problem but you're not the answer. Anyway, the second principle is not enough to change me the Holy Spirit cannot take from me what I won't release to him. He won't work without my consent. He can't remove my defects without my willingness. Because that would be violating my free will. In asking God to heal me I am commiting to the choice to be healed. This means I choose to change, I then begin that process by doing the 12steps. My ego resists this intensely the ego is afraid of change, until the choice is made to do it differently, I just keep going around in circles, Actual change occurs because of a decision to heal and change. When I decide I want to heal, I ask God to help me. I need power to change because in the past I have chosen the way of anger. Today I choose the way of love. When I accept the atonement, the correction of my perceptions I am returned to who ideally I am. All illusions will be undone and I am a son of God.

DECEMBER-2011

Peace is the result of retraining my mind to accept life as it is, rather as I think it should be. When I am not feeling peaceful, it is the result of an error in my thinking. I learn to not let anyone who does not come in peace into my territory. I read this advice avoid loud and aggressive people they are vexations to the spirit they keep me away from my peace. I do not have to give my power away I simply choose peace. I am an instrument when I choose to use my mind only for peaceful thoughts even towards those I dislike. The people who push my buttons are my greatest teachers. Why because they are teaching that I have yet to master myself. I am still on the path to enlightenment. This path involves many lessons and I must remain open to learn them. Because of my problem with booze, I been blessed to get on the path of 12-step recovery this is a better way and a piece of heaven on earth.

DECEMBER-2011

Only GODS plan for my salvation will work, part of that plan is I continue to attend 12step recovery meetings. I then decide to follow the course of action by doing the 12 steps with my sponsor. I then achieve sobriety. I am no longer a arms length away from a drink I am 12 steps away from that drink as long as I stay in fit spiritual condition. When I surrendered my life to GOD, it's like letting God be the sculptor and I became the clay, the clay has to stay moist so it can be worked with if it dries out it cant be worked with. That's how I have to be for God like moist clay because if I am rigid and attached to getting results and having things the way I think they should be I am like the dry clay unworkable. God is the director of my life, I must follow instructions my desire is to serve god. Anyway I must remember 2 key points. Gods plan works, and mine doesn't. A course I took says I need add nothing to his plan, but to recieve it. I must be willing not to substitute my own in place of it. Anything I do must be for a higher purpose I say this this prayer before I make a move. Dear GOD I surrender this situation to you may it be used for your purpose. I ask only that my heart be open to give and receive love. May all the results unfold according to your will and plan. Amen—whatever I do—I do it for GOD.

DECEMBER-2011

Here is a story a great Buddhist monk moved around naked except for a loincloth and a golden bowl, it was a gift from the king, who was a disciple. One night he was about to lie down to go to sleep. He was in a monastery when he noticed a thief lurking behind one of the columns. Here take this said the saint said holding out the golden bowl that way you won't disturb me once I have fallen to sleep. The thief eagerly took it, and ran off. Only to return the next morning with the bowl and a request. He said when you gave away this bowl so freely you made me feel very poor. Teach me how to acquire the riches that make this kind of lighthearted detachment possible.

DECEMBER-2011

Because of my past, I had an extremely negative mind. I always said that if I don't have hope then I can't get hurt again, also if I don't expect anything good then I won't be disappointed when it doesn't happen. With all the devastating things that happened in my childhood, I learned this philosophy. I was afraid to believe that anything good could happen. Since my thoughts and my mouth was all negative so was my life. When I started to study the Bible and the big book, I began to trust God that he could restore me. I realized I had to get rid of this negative outlook about life. God has a perfect plan for my life. I must learn to speak and think in agreement with his plan for my life. And if I am not sure what is his will I say well I don't know Gods plan but I know he loves me. Whatever he does will be good and I will be blessed. A scripture says all things work together for good. In Romans Apostle Paul says readily adjust ourselves to people and things. The idea is that I must learn to become the kind of person who plans things and that I don't fall apart if the plan doesn't work. I have had my fair share of success and also failure. I realize there is a lesson in both I put my trust in the king of the universe he will guide me through all hardships and pain and I will be taken care of I am under divine guidance and love. GOD is great.

DECEMBER23-2011

When I received JC as my personal savior. THE Holy Spirit came to dwell in me. The Holy Spirit knows the mind of GOD. Since the spirit knows gods mind, one of its purpose is to reveal GODS wisdom and revelations to me. That wisdom is imparted to my spirit, as a believer I am both spiritual and natural. The natural man doesn't always understand the spirit. THE holy spirit desires to bring enlightment. However when my mind is too busy with noise I can't hear it. The mind should not be filled with reasoning, worry, anxiety, and fear. However, it should be calm, quiet, and serene. My mind should be in a calm normal state. Imagine 2 people in a room together, one is trying to whisper a secret to the other, if the room is filled with loud noise and even though the message is being told the one waiting for the secret information will miss it. Because the room is too noisy, he can't hear. That is the way it is with communication between gods spirit and my spirit. THe ways of the Holy Spirit are gentle, and most of the time he speaks in a still small voice. IT is vital I keep myself in a condition conducive to hearing. My mind should be kept peaceful. As the prophet Isaiah tells us when the mind is stayed on the right things, it will be at rest.

DECEMBER-25-2011

John Lennon sings and so this is Christmas and a happy new year. What have I done with my life 2011 is almost over. I accept my gains and losses and I am looking ahead with hope to a blessed and abundant 2012. I can look back to my family and Christmas day in the Bronx and Bergenfield. I would say the last time we were all together for Christmas was in 1971inBergenfield I was 14 THE kanes my family my mother my father my sister and 2 brothers was being destroyed by alcoholism. MY family had trouble and so did I. I was 15 in 1972 it was the first time I got arrested for a burglary it wouldn't be the last I was drunk a lot angry, and out of control. Alcoholism is a family illness and my father Harold Kane died in 1979 at age 56 as a direct result from his drinking. I am sober over 10years and I am 54, I don't have to follow in my fathers footsteps. GOD and AA have done for me what I couldn't do for myself. Today is CHRISTMAS it's the day we celebrate Jesus CHRIST. JC gave up his life for me he died on that cross for all my crimes. He had 2 thieves on crosses next to him, one made fun of him the other one asked Jesus to take him with him to his kingdom. JESUS said he would. I would like to think that guy was me. My ticket to Heaven is secure by the blood ofJC I am washed clean and the many stains I had from my physical abuse and the pain of being raped by a man GOD has removed the pain and stain the mental anguish and torment also the self blame and disgrace GOD is great and his grace has given me a new mind My victory is secured and I am part of GODS family he adopted me. I have asked God the father to direct my life and help overcome all obstacles in my life. CHRISTMAS DAY-211-A loving and forgiven letter to the man, that raped me when I was 7.IT was on the Bronx side of the Harlem river on the railroad tracks it was 1964I want you to know I don't hate you I have prayed for good things for you. I did hate you for a long time I blamed you for a lot of wrong things in my life. I forgive and I love you, I realize you were sick and you didn't know what you were doing. I am writing this on Christmas day in2011-it was in1964 that you did that crime to me. I hope you are well and you got help. Jesus will forgive you if you ask him. I now accept what happened as a blessing and one of my greatest teaching tools. IHAVE learned to accept what happened was wrong and I don't blame myself, I am free from the past I have learned to release all bitterness and hatred towards you I have at times wished a painful death for you I don't feel that today I have love compassion and understanding. I take my whole life as a blessing and I did forgive and pray for you over 10years ago GOD has put it in my heart and mind last night to love you. I never would have done that myself. GOD wants me to recognize we are all one family the human family GOD is your father too our father blesses all his children

DECEMBER-2011

There were once four learned and accomplished men. They were on their way to go visit the king. Now among these men three were brilliant the fourth was far inferior in intellect, but he was the one with the most common sense. ON the road they came upon a dead lion. Let us bring the lion back to life this will bring great fame. Three of them agreed, the fourth one said if you bring this lion back to life, he will attack and devour you. One of them said don't interrupt, they were about to breathe life into the lion, when the fourth one said we should think of safety they told him to shut up they were thinking only of the fame it would bring them. Anyway, the fourth man decided to go sit in a tree just in case, The lion came back to life and killed the three wise men. The only one who survived was the man with common sense.

DECEMBER-29-2011

I cannot have a positive life and a negative mind. I have to get my thinking in line with God's word. When I have wrong negative thoughts, I am not walking in the spirit. I must renew my mind with GOD like thinking. My life is in a state of chaos from all the years of wrong thinking I cannot straighten out my life until my mind gets straight. If I want freedom, I will ask GOD for a lot of help and I will do it often. The Holy Spirit is my helper, and I lean on him, because I cannot make it alone. It is vital necessity that my thinking be right. Just as my physical life is dependent on my vital signs. And so my spiritual life is dependent upon spending regular quality time with GOD. The Bible says that a tree is known by its fruit. The same is true in my life. My thoughts bear fruit, when I think good thoughts the fruit in my life will be good, and when think bad thoughts the fruit in my life will be bad. I heard it said, where the mind goes the man follows. When I came back into 12-step recovery, my mind was obsessed with drinking alcohol. I have been set free of that addiction. However I am working on getting the impure thoughts out of my mind. And I intend to live by the the standards of purity, honesty, unselfishness and love I will continue to work towards this goal I haven't accomplished that, I am on the right path 12 steps is the way and when I change my thinking then my actions will change my insides will match my outsides I will then have integrity.

DECEMBER-2011

HEALING FROM THE SEX ABUSE-I now know I was a victim of a crime. Rape is a crime and I was only 7 when it happened. When I overcame my denial I became a survivor. I had to have courage to overcome this, and I am glad I survived long enough to get help GOD found me and I was a mess I wanted the mental torment to stop. Jesus said that his path was for me to have the good things of life and not the evil things. He wanted to redeem my lifePSALM-103-says who redeems your life from the pit who crowns you with love and kindness and also compassion, who satisfies your years with good things so that your youth is renewed like the eagle. There are many steps to restoration, the more I overcame the more peace I experienced in my life. GOD promised in Jeremiah-30-for I will restore your health and I will heal you of all your wounds GOD was healing my hurts disappointments, my failures and I was no longer an outcast. I don't feel dirty anymore. God restored my dignity I have changed how could I now be affected by what people said because I know what God said I was a overcomer I was no longer broken I feel no shame. GOD gave me back my innocence. I have joy inside of me and a believe that even when victory is delayed I still have hope in GOD. With God all things are possible.

DECEMBER-31-2011

The Tao says a structure over 9 stories high begins with a single brick also a journey of a thousand miles begins with a single step. MY journey with sobriety began by stopping drinking for one day. Along this path I also discovered peace and contentment. IN my old life I have been at war with myself and others. I lived in a world of competition, confrontation and mounting frustration. I was driven by the fear that I was not good enough, I have been sober a little while, when I got this book about the Tao, it offers inner and outer peace. The Tao says to take responsibilities for my life, and to follow the path of action and contemplation. When I shift my attitude I can experience greater peace and by seeing the larger patterns I can take effective action right now. When I have conflict in my life, I can overcome by first shifting my attitude and realizing it doesn't matter what the situation is about, but the way I perceive it. When I learn to think holistically seeing my part in the unity of life. And how we all come from one source I respect the natural cycles of life. Tao people are natural problem solvers and when I am not afraid of conflict, because I understand conflict is natural, and that life constantly goes through cycles of change. I can resolve an issue like the Tao says—wise people seek solutions, and ignorant people cast blame. And even in the conflict, I can have peace. I can relax and take a deep breath and breathe in peace and then let it flow through my entire body. Also the Tao says all life embodies yin, embraces yang, and through their union achieve harmony. Because of creative wisdom I learn that when I face a dilemma I can look beyond it because there are always more than 2 alternatives. I learn I can become like the bamboo it has strength and its graceful, upright and strong. And because it bends with the wind, it doesn't break. When I am flexible, resourceful and open to new possibilities, I become like the Tao. I am then strong in any situation, when I avoid pride and being rigid I then adjust to changes, I then harmonize and grow and also I learn that when I am hard and rigid I consort with death. And so when I am soft and flexible I affirm a greater life. I can see crisis as an opportunity to learn to become like the bamboo I can bend and grow and adjust to the winds of change. I can look within take stock of my life and set new goals Theres a old saying when one door closes another one opens I can recognize that door because I am open to new possibilities. When I follow the Tao, I live in harmony and I cultivate character. Tee and Tao are the ways of life abandon either and live in confusion because life is dynamic like a river it constantly flows. To follow Tao is to flow like a river. There is an old saying, as it is within, so it is without I develop greater character by turning within and then I release my potential and flow with nature. I can become centered, creative, and dynamic, When I listen to the inner voice and follow the call of my soul. I can demonstrate how high my human spirit can reach. I can become a self actualized human being l can show my gratitude for life by staying sober and I show my love for life by helping others achieve sobriety.

JANUARY-1-2012

Happy new year to everyone I have a lot of hope. I went to bed sober and I woke up sober. I am at the 7am meeting. I show my gratitude for being sober by helping others. We stay sober, and I get drunk, and when we became me I got drunk. And I threw away over 12 years of dry time. Today I am living a good sober life I am still growing up I have matured I need to keep going forward in my journey I lean on GOD and he has guided me into many places for the extra help I needed. I do intend to celebrate 11years of sobriety on June20th. I follow the 12 steps and I live them in my life today. I am very happy and grateful to be in recovery. This journey is long and it has many winding roads as the weather changes the seasons come and go my life is like that. I have learned not to resist change I go with the flow it's much easier I got sick and tired of the old life. I want to live for a higher purpose. GOD is love and so am I. I am a child of the king of the universe and I am loved. I share my love and sobriety with others my sobriety is a gift of love from the creator

DECEMBER-2011

A preacher put this question to a class of children. If all the good people in the world were red, and all the bad people green what color would you be? Little Linda thought for a moment then she said reverend I be streaky. Somewhere in each of us, is a mixture of light and darkness, also love and hate, also trust and fear. I have come to understand that there are ups and downs in this life and it's true that within each person there is a light within our darkness, and good within our evil because I am a imperfect human being I have learned to accept I am neither angel or beast I am both. My brokenness has allowed me to become whole. A rabbi said no one is as whole as he who has a broken heart and to experience sadness, despair, tears and howls of pain demonstrates the ultimate spirituality of acceptance. Here is a story, a young salesman approached the farmer and began to talk about this book, this will tell you everything you need to know about farming the young man said it will tell you when to sow and when to reap. It also tells about the weather, what to expect and when to expect it. This book tells you all you need to know. Young man the farmer said that's not the problem, I know everything that is in that book my problem is doing it. I have found this to be true in my life I can know the big book and the 12and 12 yet I have to take action by doing it and practicing what I have learned in life.

DECEMBER-2011

A survivor of the holocaust who received the Nobel peace prize for his writings. They showed the profound experience and the spirituality of the Jewish people. HE spoke these words at the award ceremony; no one is more capable of gratitude as one who has emerged from the kingdom of night. We know that every moment, is a moment of grace, every hour an offering, And not to share them would mean to betray them. Our lives no longer belong to us alone they belong to all those who need us desperately. And so that is why I swore never to be silent whenever and wherever human beings endure suffering and humiliation, we must always take sides. Because neutrality helps the oppressor never the victim. Silence encourages the tormentor never the tormented. That is why I have joined a group that speaks out about childhood sex abuse and it is called survivors speak up.

JANUARY-5-2012

As a child of God, I accept myself as I am. I don't waste time in self criticism, I want to see clearly and the Tao says those who know they do not know gain wisdom. And also those who acknowledge there weakness become strong, wisdom and power follow truth. For truth is the way to freedom. As in nature everything is valuable and has its place. Only human beings suffer from low self-esteem, by compulsively proving ourselves it only clutters our lives. And with self-acceptance comes peace and also humility. When I am centered in the spirit neither criticism or flattery upset me, and the judgment of others does not disturb me when I know who I am, when I follow the Tao teaching and it says the Tao person detached and wise embraces all as Tao. Detachment doesn't mean I don't give a damn and turn a cold shoulder to the world, no it means transcending the ego, and caring without getting caught up in the day to day commotion and watching life change with patience, acceptance, and good humor. And Tao people never try they do Here is a story a man walking to the center of the room dropped his pen and he repeatedly bent down trying to pick it up, I'm trying but the pen remained on the floor. Then he stood back and said don't try do it he then snatched the pen up in his hand and the lesson was very clear. Because trying is only a half hearted attempt, as was the case in my own life when I didn't live by the 12 steps, I went back to drinking after 12 years of no booze in my life I learned it was because of a halfhearted effort I only practiced 2steps in my life however I learned from my experience. And I embrace all 12 steps and I live them in my life right now and I am not afraid to make mistakes, I learn lessons even when I fail. My sobriety is a gift and I appreciate and cultivate it on a daily basis. So when I give loving service I attain fulfillment.

JUNE-2010

LOOKING BACK IS LOOKING FORWARD–My journey is to fulfill a purpose, and it is to survive life and serve GOD. I serve God by serving his people. I am here to perfect my soul. To do that I must survive and the ultimate is to be able to keep standing and make it through to the end. I do not give up cave in or give in to despair. Despair is a killer, so the meaning of life is service. A day not doing something good for someone is a day lost. Anyway are my actions for a higher good. I can reach the pinnacle of being spiritual by not letting that stop me, and also not making what the world does to me so important. This is one of the hard lessons I had to learn. It is so simple I care for the majority of people and I hope they care for me and if they don't there are others who will. And that makes me more spiritual. I quiet down my mind and know that GOD within and without, takes care of all things and my discipline is mostly behavioral how I deal with life is based upon acceptance. Most of my problems arise because I push against life, instead of going with it. When I begin to allow myself to flow and stop resisting my life is smoother and easier when I allow God to run the universe I have no problems and my life is great and a gift.

JUNE-5-2010 TRANSFORMATION

My transformation begins when I renew myself in daily meditation; I have discovered a deep source of inner peace. Those who focus on God will be one with GOD. those who study its power, will also be powerful, and those who focus on failure will certainly fail SO I get what I cultivate in life and my thoughts are like seeds they take root in my experience I can transform my world by transforming my attitude because I can't accomplish peace by reading or thinking about it, I must live my life for God by following the path with heart, so when I am confused and uncentered I project conflict into the world. And when I am at peace with myself, I can see more clearly and act more effectively. Also in this state, I am balanced, responsible, and peaceful and I radiate peace to all people. Regular meditation restores my inner harmony and also my vital energy. There is an old Chinese saying the tortoise is good at nurturing energy so it can survive a century without food and so I cultivate inner peace by setting aside time to meditate. THE disciples were absorbed in a discussion about LAO-TZU-those who know do not say, those who say do not know, and so when the master entered, they asked him what the words meant which of you know the fragrance of a rose? All of them knew, he then said put it into words all of them were silent.

DECEMBER-2010 RECOVERY FROM SEX ABUSE

I have found more memories of sex abuse I was maybe 5 or6 its very hazy and I am in a dark room a man is there he is putting something in my mouth I don't want it he makes me do it I am not sure who it is. I can also recall being on the tracks by the Harlem River it was early in the evening and it was dark the man got behind me my pants were down he hurt me I never cried or said a word Kanes don't cry i. *remained silent for over40years. So these2 people stole my childhood, and they also damaged and shattered my esteem all my early sexual contacts were with men, they were forced on me. And because of this I had great shame i am not a homo or bisexual anyway in the past I have had loveless anonymous sex with she male prostitutes., I was confused by my behavior. Because I like women and I have had 4 girlfriends in my entire life I really like some of the women at the 12 step meetings. Because I am still recovering from being raped GOD is restoring me slowly. ONE thing I learned as a child was to not be there in my mind I was somewhere else they call that dissocation. As I got older I became very confused about my sexuality, and so I have asked JC to decide for me. Because of the facts from my past I have been sick and I act out by watching porn I live in a fantasy world this is very sad. However, I do have hope because GOD promised in Jeremiah 30-17-to restore my health and heal all my wounds so most of my life I have been an outcast. GOD is healing my wounds I am no longer an outcast. I don't feel dirty inside and people don't have the power to make me feel dirty GOD has restored my dignity. And I am becoming an overcomer, I am no longer broken I feel no shame or condemnation. GOD will give me back my innocence Anyway*

I walk this long road this journey is tough I still get depressed, I do get impatient with my progress and once in a while I feel like giving up of course I won't give in because I have taken the risk of placing my recovery in his hands, I have hope that he will restore me because God is my hope. When muddy water is stilled, it becomes clear and when my mind is stilled it becomes clear be still and know that I am GOD—Richard do not be afraid GOD is with you and he is love.

DECEMBER-2011

IT is Sunday, one week to Christmas. It is the birth of JESUS CHRIST he came to save the world. And he died for my wrongdoing. JC is my big brother and my savior he heals all my wounds, he is a comforter he came for the brokenhearted I am sure he came for me. I am working again construction is slow and I haven't worked much this year. The laborers union is going through some tough times and I am looking forward to a better 2012. I am getting my second book published we are working out a few small problems with the manuscript. I am very grateful for the gift of sobriety and I do intend to celebrate 11 years of sobriety in June. I am learning to trust God with everything. I must get out of the way and let GOD be GOD When I do this I get all my needs met. I still have some lessons I gotta learn about money and business I must learn not to act on impulse and I gotta ask GOD for direction. I gotta stick with my strength and continue to work on improving my writing. This is my gift from God, and I must use it for the glory of GOD. I have to get my mind renewed on a daily basis. GOD is in charge not me, I gotta believe like it says in JOHN-316-I benefit when I think about Gods word the more time I spend meditating on the word the more I will benefit from it. When I study Gods word I am blessed with virtue and knowledge. The Bible says if I want to be a success and to prosper I must meditate on the word of GOD day and night. I needed to change my thinking because my mind was a mess. And I was thinking all the wrong things. I must never forget that my mind plays an important role in my victory. I needed to have my mind renewed to GODS way of thinking I should take a daily inventory and ask what have I been thinking about. I can choose happy thoughts, I can have my attitude improve by becoming more positive I can count my blessings. I need to know what condition my mind is in. My mind changes and at times I am peaceful and calm and at other times anxious and worried. There has been times when I believed GOD and other times when doubt and unbelief haunted me. I began to wonder when my mind is normal. Because a critical, judgmental and suspicious mind should be considered abnormal. AND I thought this type of thinking was normal because I was use to it. My mind is not reborn with the new birth experience, it has to be renewed. The renewal is a process and it takes time. AS I began to get more serious about my relationship with the lord he revealed to me that most of my problems were rooted in wrong thinking so I felt overwhelmed when I seen how much wrong thinking I still have. I would try to cast down my wrong thoughts and it would work for awhile, and then they would come back Little by little I was gaining freedom inch by inch I am going to make this garden grow I am talking about my life progress not perfection because the word of GOD teaches me that I have the mind of Christ.

DECEMBER-2011

AS I continue to grow up I realize that my impure thoughts lead to impure behavior. I must recognize this, and then change my thoughts to pure thoughts. I do continue to take inventory; because of this practice I have grown of course there is room for more growth. This journey never ends. I must continue to do self searching I have many issues the solution is always the same more spiritual growth. IN this life I have traveled many dead end streets, also I been on the road to nowhere just like the Beatles song a real nowhere man making all my nowhere plans lead me to gang life, alcoholism, jails, cocaine and crimes also loveless sex. All these left me empty and alone. I have been blessed by Gods grace so my problems are no greater than anyone else's. GOD is the answer he has all solutions. Because I am a child of GOD all things will pass also I am a new creation in JC so I am like a new born baby anyway I still stumble and fall I simply pick myself up, sometimes I learn the lesson. My restless soul is the problem. I have learned to rest inJC because I still have much to learn and that is good I remain teachable for that I am grateful, for even my difficulties because they are my greatest teachers and I am blessed when I get to the other side because the light is there and it guides me now that I am healed I can help others with the same problems we walk together in this journey.

JANUARY-10-2012-TRUTH

The ultimate truth is truth that is true now, and always has been and will be forever true. The absolute truth—is that we are unlimited beings our knowledge is unlimited so is power and joy. I begin with this thought I then direct my mind towards that will free and liberate me from sorrow and unhappiness. This leads to happiness, so when my feeling of happiness is developed fully, I then enter into a state of bliss, tranquility, and serenity. THE only authority for truth is truth and not man. My goal is self realization, I realize I am a spiritual being having a temporary physical human experience. AS I grow in my journey I do realize I am a child of God, who is on the way to becoming a son of GOD, I am still growing up. I know my life is peaceful and harmonious and I am one with everything. I balance the forces of yin and yang, I harmonize with nature and all others in my world.

JANUARY-2012

The best definition for happiness is peace, tranquility, and serenity. Happiness is the absence of apathy, grief, fear, jealousy, anger and hate. Happiness is being me without any negativity, so a attitude of giving makes one happy. I seek out periods of silence. I find peace this way. Gandhi kept a day of silence once a week, most of us can't keep a whole day of silence. However I can establish regular periods of meditation, I like to meditate I think of the waves on the water I put my problems on the out waves I let the in waves bring peace I do this over and over, until my mind slows down, So after meditation I emerge renewed and refreshed most of my tension is gone I am at peace, and one with God. I also empty my heart because it's necessary to remove the blocks to inner peace. Anyway it's impossible to be at peace when I am in conflict with another person, I release grudges and negative feelings, I then reclaim peace of mind. Emptying my heart and daily meditating will build inner strength, I will find myself growing more balanced and more at peace with the world. I recognize the power of my thoughts, I use this power wisely, I then find the source of peace within. I express my peace to others, I respect the process, I then harmonize with nature, and all others in my world. The way of peace begins with self acceptance. Because when I accept myself I naturally accept others, the essential lesson is my outer world reflects my inner world. *The future of the world lies in having enough self-esteem to accept others different from ourselves. It's up to me to learn how to use my power for life rather than death. I renew my faith and live each day in a way that can truly lead to a world of peace, and as a child of GOD I can dare to be open, I can reach out to others to create greater understanding I gotta believe I can make the world a better place by becoming a better person I can treat everyone with equal respect.*

JANUARY-2012

I cannot be open with others unless I first accept myself. My low self-esteem builds walls of defensiveness, and this keeps me from the peace I seek. Anyway, because of my insecurity I hide behind walls I am afraid to relax and be myself, so this only increases my insecurity, because I think putting up walls keeps me save. This is not true because the more I hide the more fearful I become. The way out begins with self-acceptance, when I stop hiding the walls gradually disappear. Building self-acceptance takes time because I have self-criticism, and it brings up past mistakes it tells me I am not good enough and scares me with worries about the future. My inner monologue tells me you did it wrong again are you stupid or you are a bad boy all of this stuff I heard in the past from parents and other people. All of this undermines my self-esteem and it makes me feel incompetent, weak and helpless. I can turn this off with affirmations like this-I love myself I accept myself I am one with GOD. I can also stop this by giving full attention to something I can do it has to be something I really love, I can take a walk by the river, I can weightlift or I can meditate. I resolve to do something I love on a regular basis, because this is a spiritual exercise. Since what I believe I create this is the power of the self-fulfilling prophesy. I can learn to love myself by looking in the mirror and telling myself Richard I really love you I do this daily and often. This regular exercise of self-approval will build my self-esteem and increase my inner peace. Fear builds walls, but truth builds bridges, this is the way of truth with greater honesty I can build bridges of peace, understanding hope and sobriety, I accept greater peace in my life now and so it is.

JANUARY-2012

Love and giving are synonymous, love is acceptance and taken people as they are. The more I develop love, the more I come in touch with the harmony of the universe and my life becomes more beautiful I begin a cycle of positive actions. My actions are constructive and it affects everything, this is why 12 step recovery meetings are so effective, because where two or more are gathered in his name he is there with us, and its sacred ground, Because we help each other stay sober, we build each other up, and we make the world a better place to live, by changing ourselves we can make a difference. Bill Wilson was voted one of the top 100men of the last century, he started AA and the 12 step movement was born it continues to grow we also have a book to teach us to live a sober contented life. This is pure love. God and 12step recovery teaches me to take charge of my life to face my fears, and learn from them. Panic is the ultimate enemy because it can damage my heart and undermine my immune system and also lead to sudden death. We can avoid panic with knowledge and foresight by anticipating emergencies a good pilot is prepared he doesn't panic in a crisis because he knows what to do. The right response becomes second nature. When I understand I make better choices like a martial arts master they see current crisis in terms of larger patterns. I use to think if I ignore danger it will go away, this is denial and is a foolish response to any problem. Because unsolved problems do not go away. I can learn how to direct my energy into posistive channels. Takeing charge means responding wisely to conditions around me andknowing when and how to act. I do this by studying the way things work I then act in harmony with them. By following GOD I gradually overcome my fear of change. I know now my mistakes bring greater wisdom. I must be willing to risk and learn through mistakes, so people with experience are those who have learned to profit from there errors. I use to rush around looking to be bigger and better, this revealed only inner emptiness, also a lack of peace. Competive thinking puts people on the defensive and I often attacked others because I percieved them through my fear I am challenged to change attack thoughts with compassion. The TAO TE CHING says when we are at peace with ourselves were not vulnerable to the attack of others. I become pure as a child, in purity is strenght, if I don't fear others they wont fear me. The wise person trusts the process this lesson I must learn again and again trust the process I cannot change the cycles of life to suit myself however I can learn to flow with them.

Richard Kane

NOVEMBER-2003 OLDER WRITINGS

The freedom of forgiveness and learning to let go also the freedom of living today. The past don't own me, I am learning to put it all in my higher powers hands. He doesn't care what happened or what I did and what I didn't do he doesn't care what I have and what I don't have because he accepts me just the way I am. And i am working on that lesson., so I am becoming a new person. I still at times miss the old life, I don't mean the drinking. I am talking about my life as a Hells Angel I have hard time letting go. I had a lot of pride, because I was part of the best and it fed my big ego. I still continue to talk about going to jail the fights and all the wasted years because I needed to feel like a tough guy. In my mind I am a stand up street guy, I knew when to keep my mouth shut and I don't talk to cops. Its very hard to let this stuff go. I am getting closer to my higher power anyway I am still a uptight person and I don't how to relax. I am getting better I have grown up because I have a relationship withGod I at times still live in a fantasy world and I have crazy thinking progress has been made, GOD and 12 step meetings fix a broken person like me.

NOVEMBER-2002

I am trying to be more posistive, and I live one day at a time, I am healing and I am getting better. Monday I go for my blood test, to see if the hepatitis c iscomeing back, I hope it isnt, and I do have some fear about this. Because I don't want to go back on that chemo medicine. I am going back to the union hall on Tuesday, I am number 17 on the out of work list, and I hope I will be going back to work real soon. Hope is very vital to me and it guides me. GOD provides all my needs. Living sober is a growing process, and right actions is the key because talk is cheap I have to practice this in all my affairs. I talk to my higher power all the time I use simple prayers like the serenity prayer, slowly I am getting better I need to listen more. Because I still have a lot of sick thinking, so I try not to listen to it. I ask GOD for the moral courage to do what is right, I continue to grow because I have done a lot of step work. I write and I let certain people read them, and I talk to a lot of people in recovery, and we talk about my problems from my childhood, I have talked about my sex problems and my criminal activity this was all part of *my old life, and I will continue to talk because it takes the power away from these things so a lot of my guilt and shame is going away because I have taken action.*

DECEMBER-2005

I do remember feeling real bad after I almost got murdered, and that was in 1995. i GOTcrushed on my motorcycle in paterson and I was left for dead. After I got released from the hospital I went back to 3rd street I lived there. I was I n a lot of pain, and I couldn't sleep, so I was taken pain pills. I was very weak full of doubt and confusedSome of my brothers from the Hells Angels were mad at me, and I was pissed at myself, and I wanted to get better so I could seek revenge. I wanted to regain my respect, I felt all alone. Some of my brothers said some pretty cruel things and I begin to think they were out to get me. I did have to get surgery on my leg, do you know the intense pain of being crushed at 40or50 miles per hour and being left to die it wasn't no scratch. IWAS voted out of the club was I really given a fair chance. I do realize I was stubborn and I made a foolish mistake I never really wanted anything to go wrong. Myfalse pride and big ego got the best of me and so I went to Paterson to put up flyers in them bars about Cochises party. Anyway I want to apologize to all my former brothers in the New York City charter. I made a very foolish decision and I never intended to hurt the club. A lot of time has passed since that dark day and I am moveing on with my life anyway for a while I did want another chance. The Hells Angels are fine with out me, and it wasn't meant to be, I did have my doubts I do now accept that I got out voted 100 percent, so in the long run it doesn't matter anymore. I have learned many lessons from my mistakes I realize all things are possible with God and I believe anything can happen so I will continue to stay sober, and I will work at becoming a better human being. I learned I cant change the past, none of us has that power I am human I have regrets and I wish that day never happened however I have learned to live with it and grow up.

Richard Kane

JANUARY-2012-

I am sustained by the love of GOD. Here is the answer to every problem. Because I believe I am sustained by everything but GOD, so my faith is placed in insane symbols like booze, money, prestige, jobs being liked and knowing the right people, rideing in a motorcycle club, this list is all forms of nothingness. and I have endowed them with magical powers, all of these are my replacements for the love of GOD. They are all about the ego, I have learned not to put my faith in the worthless it will not sustain me. Only the love of GOD will protect me in all circumstances. It will lift me out of every trial, and raise me high above all percieved dangers of this world into a climate of perfect peace and safety. Because I am a son of GOD I have eternal calm. I don't put my faith in illusions they will always fail me. I put all my faith in the love of GOD. Because this love is changeless, eternal, and it never fails. This is the answer to whatever confronts me. Through the love of God i resolve all difficulties without effort and in total confidence, Because I have learned to rest in GOD so this thought brings me the peace, stillness and safety I seek This thought has the power to awakeing the sleeping truth in me. So when I rest in GOD this will carry me through the storms, strife past miseries and pain, and there is no suffering it cannot heal. Also there is no problem it cannot solve. This is the day of peace so I rest in God while the world is torn apart by the winds of hate, I remain completely undisturbed because I rest in the truth. Because I gave my voice to GOD I let him speak through me. I am a instrument for peace, and I want to bring peace to this dark violent world. Because we are all one family violence doesn't solve problems and it always starts another cycle of revenge. Love is the answer. GOD is love we are all created in his image we are the world and we are love so lets all of us pull together for the highest good. I have been blessed with sobriety I intend to celebrate 11 of sobriety in june. Also I am in remission from hepatitis c for more than 9 years what a miracle. GOD is in the miracle business. Ibelieve GOD healed me, and he sent ArchAngel Rapheal and Micheal and other Gaurdian Angels to help me. This is very strange because I am a former HellsAngel talk about irony. I am being helped by heaven I am being transformed and I am a messenger for GOD and 12 step recovery groups. I continue to pray to Heaven and Raphael they respond to my prayers I do have to ask for help because they cant violate my free will and assist me with out my permission. I can pray for healing and after I pray I let go of worrying or trying to control how it will be answered. I instead trust in GODS amazing wisdom and love, and he *will create a custom made solution so I let Heaven surprise me in the way it answers my prayer. Dear ARChANGEL RAPHEAL I ask that you soothe my mind and nerves with your emerald green light, help me to relax and trust that I am safe and protected.*

JANUARY-14-2012-

When I seek simplicity I can overcome selfishness, and my wasteful desires. Anyway what was more wasteful in my life than my drinking. Today I keep it simple and I live by the 12 steps. So I no longer need to drink booze. So chaseing desires can drive me mad, when I seek inner wisdom I then let go of excess. This affirms the truth, and the truth sets me free. I seek the silence and there is where I find GOD. I am sustained by the love of God. Here is something from the Tao, great trouble comes from not knowing what is enough, and great conflict arises from wanting to much. My drinking got out of control and I couldn't stop on my own. I asked God to take the obsession for booze out of my life, and he has done that. He replaced one spirit booze is called spirits, and he gave me his spirit. When seeking knowledge much is aquired, when seeking Tao much is discarded. The Tao says not to let anyone do our thinking, because they study life and they listen to others. They weigh there options but they make there own decisions. They follow inner guidance and they seek silence. Because much chatter brings only exhaustion, so stay true to your center. Close your mouth shut your doors and live close to Tao. Open your mouth be busy all day and live in confusion. Anyway I must stay centered I want to bring greater peace to my life and the world. I simplify life by getting rid of unecessary possessions I comminicate simply and honestly and I use my time wisely.-HEALING MY WOUNDS_GOD how can you mend a broken heart, when I was a boy I had a open heart however I learned very young to close my heart. The reason was the violence done to me by my father, I would get punished and beating for the simplest things. So I learned how to mask the pain, I went into a fantasy world durieng the beating. I learned how not to move or express any emotion, because I knew I wouldn't get beating as much and it would end much sooner. Anyway this was my reality as a child. So I built emotional defenses, and I learned to build a fortress across my heart I had a hard heart I became a survivorHowever as I got older I devoloped a loser mentality. So I joined a street gang with the name

Born Losers. I understand the law of atrraction works both ways so I got back what I put out into the universe. So when I put out negative energy what else can I expect I reaped what I sown. I must get rid of these illusions. I can access my higher self and with awareness start working on changing these thoughts to positive ones. Although the experience of the trauma of being raped as a child can lead me to deviate from my true nature, I realize the HolySpirit will hold and guide me until I choose to return to love because GOD is love and he doesn't see me the way I think he does, he sees me as his son unblemished, worthy and loveing.

JANUARY-15-2012

My thoughts are images I have made. I think I see them, and this is how my seeing was made. This is the function I have given my bodys eyes and this is not seeing its image making, it takes the place of seeing replacing vision with illusions. Be still and know that I am GOD. So I can discover my center of peace. The Tao teaches that without the center life means nothing. So it is not what we look like or what we do but what we are that brings meaning and purpose. The ocean is a marvelous symbol of TAO its vast, fluid, and constantly moveing beneath its turbulent surface is the quiet depths. So beneath the restless surface of my life, lies a deep source of peace, power and inspiration. I can find this deep center in meditation or reflection. I come to realize my job is not my center, because who I am is always more than what I do. When I learn to detach from externals I affirm my center and I am one with GOD. I am centered whole and complete I have a job but I am not my job, I have a family but I am not my family, I have relationships but im not my relationships I also have a body but im not my body and so I have learned I am one withGOD I respect myself and the process of getting better through the 12 steps of recovery.-january-affirmations-2012-I give and receive tender loveing care, count my blessings-I matter—I can make a difference-I trust the higher power—I pray—one day at a time, one thing at a time, easy does it, do it now, be loveing kind and gentle-be willing-let go—show care concern compassion—I believe have faith—I have hope—I grow-be honest—I am a hardworker-reliable—I have peace health and harmony—I have abundance, I am blessed, I share and I give back, I am richly blessed—I am grateful, I thank my higher power for everything—I live sober-I think sober—I walk the walk—I am growing, I am glowing, I believe in the light I give thanks I believe in the highest good, my sobriety is the most important thing in my life today

JANUARY 2012-AFFIRMATIONS

I am now releasing my past. All my negative self images and attitudes are now being dissolved, I love and appreciate myself, the light within me is creating miracles in my body, mind, and affairs, I am now creating my life exactly as I want it, I accept myself completely here and now. I am now willing to experience all my feelings because none of my feelings are negative they are all important parts of who I am. its okay for me to have fun, I enjoy being sober, I love my freedomand I deserve to be healthy and feel good. I give thanks for ever increasing health, beauty, and vitality. God is the unfailing, unlimited source of all my supply. Abundance is my true state of being, I am now ready to accept it fully and joyfully.

JANUARY 2012

I must continue to purify my thinking because I want to leave behind my toxic ways of thinking. Because I know my thoughts lead to my actions, so I must become very careful about my thoughts, and I understand my thoughts can poison my life. My ego is the problem and I must continue to reduce the ego. I can access my higher awareness by getting rid of doubt, cultivating the witness and shutting down inner voices. I must begin to recognize and change toxic thinking to pure thinking. I want to be free from my ego, I must be willing to confront the ways I have been thinking. This is the beginning of the purification process. I need to know that I can choose less toxic thoughts, this is a important insight, and I am on a sacred path. I know that who I am is something grander than the thoughts I think, and I am more divine than my body where my thoughts occur. My thoughts and behaviors are habits anyway to purify my thinking and make my mind work exactly as I want, I examine these habits and thoughts. Then I begin the process and work towards returning to the sacred self.

JANUARY-2012-SEXUAL IDENTITY

The Tao tells us develop your masculine power yet be gentle and nuturing become open like a valley so the river of virtue flows through you returning me to source. In traditional cultures men are active and aggressive this is yang, and women are submissive this is yin, we each possess both tendencies. Anyway opposites attract so as we mature we seek this opposite within ourselves in a process called indivvation. In seeking out this unconscious potential we balance yin and yang. Becoming more whole, more complete more at peace. So the wisdom of Tao leads beyond narrow definitions. Men and Women of Tao are gentle and strong, patient and assertive and follow there own energies and respond appropiately to situations. My higher self urges me to view a woman as a soul who has a body. My ego is determined that I see her as a physical body, and my libido represents my basic sexual desires, this is vital and not viewed with scorn or contempt. However when my libido becomes the controlling influence in how I use my mind, my thinking can become toxic and drift from the bliss and harmony that my sacred self offers, so to purify my thoughts in this area I will have to carefully examine all that I learned about my sexual nature. And when I look at the beliefs I grew up with about male sexuality I realize I was exposed to toxic thinking. These beliefs interfered with my spiritual development. Most of the messages I got taught me to relate to a female as a physical body, and the goal was the conquest of her body. The reason this kind of thinking becomes toxic, it uses up so much energy as has me viewing females as bodies rather than spiritual beings. Relationships then become focused on apperance and external beauty and having sex becomes a subsitute for love and being spiritual partners. So when I am motivated by my libido my thoughts are overwhelming because I constantly think about sexual things. So I had this realization that I can allow my higher self to be the force in my life and what I do to free myself is to see the inner beauty that is in each and everyone of us In my own case because all my early sexual contacts where with men that forced themselves on me I was under 10 years old in every incident I have asked GOD to heal me from this burden I had immense inner pain and turmoil I struggled with my identity I developed a hatred for sexual things I felt they were dirty and evil I was very sick I mean being raped at 7 years old really screwed me up I am on the right path and I becoming whole I am healed GOD is going restore me to what I really am one day I will have a girlfriend I am being purified in Gods time. I say these things daily, I love myself, I accept myself and I am one with God. I am sustained by the love of GOD

JANUARY AFFIRMATIONS

The more I outflow the more space I create for good things to come to me. I am now putting my life in order preparing to accept all the good that is comeing to me. I give thanks now for all the good that I have and all the good things to come. I am now releasing my past and I now forgive and release everyone in my life. I am now letting go of all accumlated guilt, fears, resentments dissapointments and grudges I am free and clear. Every day I am growing healthier and more attractive. I am growing stronger and more powerful. I love my body as it is. I have strenght, wisdom, serenity, compassion, softness, warmth, clarity, intelligence, creativity, and healing power.

JANUARY 2012

I get up in the middle of the night I go outside and I look at the sky. i see the moon and the stars its so awesome what beauty in the universe, and so I think I can reach out and touch the stars of course I cant. I am a piece of the universe. God made all this and it all works in perfect harmony. Anyway in the daytime I go for walks by the river. I look at the blue sky the sun and the clouds and once in a while I see a rainbow. The energy in the universe and nature is powerful and gentle. I go along on my peaceful walk I know I am connected to all of this and I am a part of the universe. The spirit in the sky is my father and the father of all creation so I am one with everybody and every other creature. This life is a blessing and being sober is my greatest blessing.

JANUARY-AFFIRMATIONS

I feel and trust the presence of the lord in my life, and everytime I release a little more of my limitations I create more space inside of me for something new. I am learning to follow the spirit where ever it wants to take me, when I do this I experience joy, power, love, peace and excitement, love waits on welcome not on time, with love in me I have no need except to extend it. Gratitude goes hand and hand with love, to love yourself is to heal yourself, to forgive is to heal yourself, peace to my brothers and sisters who are one with me, I teach only love for that is what I am.

JANUARY-20-2012

*This is a new year how am I doing? I am staying sober, and I do plan on celebrating 11 years on June 20*th*. Anyway I am turning 55 on June 5th. Life goes by so quick. I got layed off from my construction job last week because of the weather everything is alright, I will wait until works starts again. I am blessed with great health and I have a positive outlook about life, and I do continue to grow in this journey. I did finish my second book, and I am working on writing my third book. I continue to grow in my relationship with GOD., also I do have a relationship with Jesus I call him JC. Because of his love I have been released of so much of the pain from the past. JC did promise he would restore to me the years the locust ate. Anyway I did find more incidents of sex abuse, and I was even younger around 5 or 6 and that was the first time and the last time was when I was 12 they were all men. I no longer care about that and I am not afraid because God and JC are healing all my wounds. these wounds are invisible no one knows about them they are old emotional scars. Yet only GOD can heal these type of wounds, so I bring them to him because he does what no one can do. He restores my soul and dignity and he makes me pure. HE gives me self worth and he tells me everything is alright and he holds and heals me. GOD sends the ArchAngels Micheal and Rapheal they are my friends and protectors. I invite them into my life, so my healing is going along at its own pace. I have great confidence in God and all the Angels and Heaven is working with me so I can get better. Anyway I don't get discouraged when I fall short I have learned to just keep striving forward, and I am experiencing joy in my life. I achieve joy by returning to my orignal nature. So when I hold to the Tao within, joy will surely follow and when I do this I don't fear exposure or ridicule. Because I know who I am I am unaffected by flattery or criticism so I can transcend the pitfalls of the ego. Anyway when I am rushed I can slow down and ask if what I am doing* *makes sense, because with haste I lose my balance, and life becomes a blur, so I can slow down and return to harmonyI have learned to let go of my violent ways because it doesn't solve problems. I know because I follow the examples of Martin Luther king andGandhi because they used non violence and achieved great things. I grew up withviolence it was done to me I used it many times in my life and I looked up to men of violence. I have changed, I am peaceful I have a purpose in this life and I want to be a person who can bring positive change to this worldI would like to see the end of violence. I can be peaceful and live in harmony with all of GODS creation.*

JANUARY-21-2012

What is the ultimate challenge for the spiritual warrior—relinquishing control. So I am askedto take a risk and a leap of faith. So I leap empty handed into the void I then let go of old behaviors, fears and defects of character. Anyway first I need to know what holds me back, and what believes that keep me from growing and becoming my true self. I then need willingness to changeI start by becoming willing to let go of old ideas, habits, and patterns. Finally I need to ask JC to remove everything that holds me back. Because I may start to worry and say what will I be? I become afraid and think no I cant do that, I must stay in charge of my world and I will hang on tighter and think my life may not be pretty but at least its familiar. So out of resitance comes willingness, and out of fear comes faith and suddenly I am free to leap I surrender and let go. So today I pray for courage to let go iwant to be happy. I walk this spiritual path because true spirituality is liberation not just from the delusions of my drinking but also from the delusions of religion. When I obtain freedom from the fear of death, a sound way of health and a path of understanding my life becomes happy and I need no false leaders. I ask—do I want salvation, and peace because I do not have them now, because my mind is undisciplined—so I cant distinquish between joy and sorrow pleasure and pain also love and fear. I am now learning how to tell them a part, and great will be my reward. My decision is all I need to start, this spiritual path leads me to the truth. AND the truth is GOD has one son, and he is the ressurection, and the life and his will is done because all power is giving him in Heaven and on earth

JANUARY-22-2012

I was brought up with the idea of how to live for tomorrow, and this is a theory of life based on fear. I am afraid of the future so I don't dare live with joy today and I am anxious. So today is for making sure tomorrow will be safeSo my life never really starts and fear runs my life the curtain never rises and the best I can hope for is a good dress rehearsal. When I got hepatitisC all that changed and I learned to live in the now I realized my attitudes and behaviors mattered and I live in this present moment. Before I got into 12 step recovery, I had been lost in a world of booze, compulsive sex and motorcycle gang life I had all but disappeared so it was time to come back. Sobriety brought me back to life, anyway getting hepatitis c, and then taken treatment I became well and that brought me back to reality. SO its time to live and to be who I always wanted to be, and to live the way I always wanted to live. I am totally alive and present so I will make my life exactly the way I want it to be. I am happy, whole, and complete. So 12step recovery is the best thing that ever happened to me. There once was a wanderer from the Bronx who cared nothing for fame, although he had many chances for that, he continued to search for teachers who could teach him to master 5 things guitar, chess, books, painting and sword. The guitar gave him music which expressed his soul. Chess cultivated strategy and a response to the actions of another. Books gave him acedemic education. Painting was the exercise of beauty and sensitivity. Sword was a means for defense. One day a little boy asked the wanderer what he would do if he lost the 5 things. At first he was frightened he soon realized that his guitar could not play itself. And the chess board was nothing without players. A book needed a reader, brush and ink could not move on its own. And a sword could not be used without a hand. He realized that his cultivation was not merely for that, and it was not just for acquiring skills, it was a path to the innermost part of his being. I remember when I came to 12 step recovery meetings someone said let us love you until you can learn to love yourself. I don't know about you this scared the hell out me I was not used to hearing this kind of stuff no one hardly ever told me that—this threw me off guard. It takes a long time to learn to love ourselves because so many things I did seem so hard to forgive and I am trying to dig out from tons of negative garbage. For tunately our friends in the program do love us and this will sustain me until I get the picture of myself back into proper focus. The thing we must get locked firmly in our minds is that its alright to be who we have been and who we are now. WE are on a journey and we know how to repare the damage, Our program shows us the way to recovery, the way back to genuine esteem because we are gods creation. God made us and always loves us just the way we areSo I will try to love myself remembering thatGOD and other people love and accept me. I have learned to surrender my life past, present, and future to Gods care and directionI listen, I accept and rely onGODS guidance and carry it out in everything I think say or do. I live in peace and harmony with the natural laws. To live in harmony is to follow Tao and, to follow this is enlightenment. Because excessive striving leads to exhaustion because of competive struggle and whatever violates that will not endure. So wars and social conflicts are symptons of a imbalanced societyTAoists have equated peace with balance. The hexagram for peace in the I Ching is made up of 3 horizontal lines divided in the center above 3 solid horizantal lines, SO the Yin of earth is balanced by theYang of Heaven. Peace results from this dynamic balance of opposites. For peace to exist societies and individuals must recognize and understand there unity with one another and nature.

JANUARY-2012

The acceptance of guilt into the mind of GODS son was the beginning of the seperation, and the acceptance of the atonement is its end. This world I see is a delusional system of those made by guilt. Look carefully at this and you will realize this is so, this world is the symbol of punishment and laws this the laws of death. GODS son is not guilty he deserves only love because he has given only love. The atonement is the final I must learn, because my ego teaches me to attack myself. I think I am guilty and I feel I must be punished. This is not so my guilty secrets are nothing and if I would bring it to the light, the light will dispel them. Then no dark cloud will remain between me and God, anyway in remebering GOD the father I will see his guiltless son who did not die because he is imortal and I will see that I was redeemed with him and I have never been seperated from him. Because of this understanding I will remember to recognize love without fear so there will be great joy in Heaven because I have come home.

JANUARY-25-2012

The ancient chinese saw each person as a microcosm of the world. They equated our heads with the heavens, our feet with earth, our veins with rivers our many bones with the 365 days of the year and our changing emotions like the changing weather. Diseases in humans like disorder in the world were caused by imbalance. I have been on a journey to discover my true sacred self. Because I have been out of balance I have experienced many extremes—I have made some poor choices iwas searching and looking for love and acceptance. So I was searhing for love and acceptance out side of myself and it eluded me. I joined a club I was one of the orignal members of the Desperadoes motorcycle club, we were a small club I became discontented so I left them. I then decided to become a Hells Angel so I went down to 3rd street and became a prospect. I did that for 18 months I became a member the honeymoon didn't last long. I found myself kicked out—what a bummer. Sometimes a bad ending is really a disguize for a new beginning. I found myself feeling defeated, but the lord of the universe came to me in my lowest moment I wanted to die he gave me strenght and he kept me alive. I must continue to grow up and face my difficulties, I am looking at them as lessons. I am working on new ways of being pure in body, mind, and spirit. Anyway when I feel myself being persuaded by the demands of my body, I can take a few moments to become silent and listen for direction from my higher self. Its in these precious few moments that I will find the strenght to forsake the demands of the ego. So even if I only do this for a moment or two, I have made progress and what I think about will eventually become habit. I give myself permissionTO think about shifting to a higher spiritual base and this will get the wheels in gear to overide the ego. I then begin keeping track of my judgemental thoughts, so I increase my awareness of this judging habit-anyway when I notice that I am having a judgemental thought about the physical appearance of someone, I then realise I can redirect my thoughts to consider the fullness of GOD in that person, as I catch myself in judgemental attitudes. I will begin to break this habit. I will eventually replace this habit with pure thoughts towards everyone I meet.

JANUARY-2012 SEXUAL ABUSE RECOVERY

My sex abuse distored my understanding so I tried to compensate for my inability to trust, and feel secure. because of my fear I isolated so I could survive I learned to avoid people and run away. When I got older I hid in a bottle of booze, and I tried to control my own life. Anyway because of my past I knew I couldn't trust, and I found out I was not in control I was living in fear. because I am a victim of a crime rape is a brutal crime. I am like a fragile flower that is being blown apart and life has attempted to destroy me by one storm after another. Even though I developed a hard heart to survive, I am still that fragile flower that's being blown apart. I have learned its never to late to get out of the storm. So I gave control to GOD and took steps to trust in him. I made a decision to forgive and it was not a one time deal. the process took a long time. I forgave the perpetrator, I forgave the betrayal of innocence, I forgave the thieves of my childhood. I forgave the shattering of my identity I forgave everything. So I began to feel better, and less angry but still empty. So I started to forgive the perpetrator each time I had a flashback—so everytime a memory would flash across my mind I would forgive and there were a lot of them. I would ask GOD to restore his love in place of despair and mental anguish, and when I became angry and overreacted I asked God to forgive me. I would ask God to replace with his love what had been taken from me. I became determined to do everything I could to believe in God. So if he could really resore me I knew I could make it through life and God will help me to get there. GOD said he would restore all the love that had been stolen and he will send away all the hurt the bitterness, the pain, anger, and the abuse. I allow GOD to replace my despair and loneliness and the betrayal with his love, joy and his blessings. I am being blessed this journey is long and difficult I don't walk alone I have the holy spirit and all my friends in recovery thanks everybody.

JANUARY-26-2012

Sexual energy is passion and feeling alive it is life and the creative force of the universe. When I trust and follow this energy, it leads me into appropiate action in any given situation. There is a time for everything even the bible says that. So there is a time to physically make love. when I am not afraid to experience and express all my feelings I come alive, I can feel everything more deeply and I can have a sense of fulfillment. I can express this energy in a natural way—so looking at a flower or having a moment of eye contact with someone can be pleasing and fulfilling and so can a physical sexual encounter. Then my life is filled with the sexuality of the universe. unfortunately I have become a master at cutting of my sexual energy and I have become afraid of it., I have learned to suppress it and this is all because of my ego. I then attempt to control or exploit what is natural. Because I still believe my sexual energy is sinful and dangerous and I distrust myself. I have the mistaken idea that spiritual and sexual energies are opposites. because I don't recognize they are the same I try to split myself I then try to deny my sexuality this creates a tremendous conflict. I end up blocking this energy. This enegy is pure and its waiting to pour through me. This unlimited power scares me and I try to control the energy instead of trusting myself with it. So I don't know what pure sexual energy would look like because I have bought into the rules or I rebelled and both of these patterns set me up and prevent me from discovering the true nature of my sexual energy. So when I set limits on my sexual energy it becomes distorted. I believe its something to be hidden ignored and controlled. I have learned to hold back or to act sexually at certain safe moments, this energy can become dead because I have blocked it. This energy is natural anyway I didn't want to get stuck in the suppresive rules I rebelled I had sex whenever and with whoever I wanted and this behavior causes the energy to die, because it does not come from the inside as this starts to die I seek more ways to stimulate and exite myself I am looking to be satisfied I end up pushing it further away and the more I try to grasp it the more it eludes me. I have to learn to get in touch with my real energy so it takes letting go of all previous ideas. it means changing everything I have to risk trusting myself and learn to put away the external rules I discover my internal rhythm, because I allowed my inhibitions and fear to rule my lifeI played it safe I was too afraid to get involved with anybody I do realize that my sexual abuse had a lot to do with this I looked at my sexuality as evil dirty vulgar and perverted so I acted on these beliefs and my behavior mirrored that. I am starting to accept who I am our big book says our sexuality is good and God given it's a gift. I must learn to use this gift in the way God wants me to, I can start a new life in this area imust let go and let GOD.

JANUARY-2012

-Loggers delight in straight grained strong fragrant wood if the timber is to difficult to cut, to twisted to be made straight or to spongy for fire wood. Only useful trees are cut down. The useless ones survive. The same is true of people the strong are conscripted the beautiful are exploited. Those who are to plain to be noticed are the ones who survive, they are left alone and safe. What if I am one of the plain ones, anyway others may neglect us, we should not think we have no value. We must not accept the judgement of others as the measure of our own self worth, instead we should live our lives in simplicity. Surely I will have flaws I must take stock of them and then use them as a measure of self improvement. I am free to cultivate the best parts of my personalitie so to be considered useless is not a reason for depair. This is a opportunity and a chance to live without interference and to express my own individuality. I recall 1995-when I got the boot from the Hells Angels I was kicked out dishonorable and I was called a coward, I thought I lost everything. I was no longer useful to them I wandered around messed up and feeling useless. Then one day after hitting a harder bottom I did consider takeing my life instead I cried out to the Lord—I cant do this anymore—please help me. I then returned to the 12 step meetings so I took this opportunity to save my own life. I discovered iwas only useful to theHells Angels when iwas strong. They exploited me and I allowed it, I thought I needed the prestige of that patchMy vision cleared and I see clearly now so my value is much more than that patch. I am a child of GOD and this is my real value. Do you remember the band Blind Faith, Eric Clapton played with them how about the song Presence of the Lord, they sang I have finally found a way to live in the presence of the lord—so have i.

JANUARY-27-2012

Blessed are the pure in heart for they shall seeGOD. Purity is simply living the way GOD wants us to live. Purity is being honest to the best of my ability about what is beneficial for me physically, mentally, and spiritually. In purity as in honesty the virtue lies in the striving as I seek the truth when I give my all in the constant pursuit of righteousness. I will be free and even though I may never reach my objective. The pursuit is a thrilling and challenging *journey. This journey is as important as the destination and even though it may seem slow I must carry on. I need to address purity in terms of mind, body, and soul. Each of us has a intuitive sense as to what is right but do we have the dedicated will to do it. I must have a determined desire to do that which I know is right, if I am going to achieve a degree of purity. Am I pure in my relations with the opposite sex. First I must acknowledge the fact of sex, to act as if there is no such thing as sex desires in me is to repress them, and a complex is set up in the subconscious this leads to nervous trouble and psychological breakdown. Since sex desires are one of our basic instincts there is no shame in this. The question is not whether we have sex desires but whether sex desire has us., as a servant of a higher purpose it's a wonderful gift giving drive and beauty to life. As a master its hell I want be to be free do I have victory or defeat or am I becoming corrupt in act or thought if so will I surrender it now. The constant pursuit of sexual gratification can become a addiction, like any addiction a obsession with sex seperates me from GOD. Because feeding the mind impurities is like feeding the body tainted food. we know the consequences of such foolishness we don't eat spoiled food. So why then do we feed the mind contaminated food that will slowly but surely destroy the soul and even though I stumble in this area I know GOD can take it away I believe withGOD I can overcome every temptation. I gotta believe GOD can keep me pure he has never allowed a soul to suffer for resisting temptation. So I must accept that watching porn and going to escorts for sex is impureand not the will of GOD. Even though I have not eliminated these behaviors I have made progress and I do intend to eliminate them completely I do want to be pure. Because some of my old ideas still excist they are in my mindI am like the Bronx wanderer I am still searching for loveand it's a delusion to look where I have been searching. GOD is the answer and the practice of prayer puts me in touch with the truth that is in me.*

JANUARY-30-2012

I am in awe when I look at the stars and the moon on a clear night, life is full of mystery and there is so much I don't understand. The universe works in perfect harmony, look at how the weather changes we have the 4 seasons. I am here to learn I must remain teachable. Because a master without a master is dangerous, We looked up to our parents there responsibility was to guide and educate us they even made judgements on our behalf until we learned to make our own decisions based on the wisdom they helped develop. Yet the potential for abuse and mistakes is very great what person can be right all the time. A simple lapse at the wrong time can cause confusion and psychological scars. Harsh words to a child can engender years of problems. That is why we need a parent for the parent and a master for the master and leaders for the leaders, because this prevents errors of power. In the past even Kings had wise advisors. Eventually someone has to be at the top So let us not invoke deities but pragmatism. It is experience that is the ultimate teacher. This is why wise people travel constantly and test themselves against the flux of circumstances. Its only in this way they can truly confirm there thoughts and compensate for there shortcomeings. Of course the ultimate teacher in my life is God. All my years of hard drinking brought me to my knees, I asked for help I surrendered I began my recovery journey. I rejoined the human race because we are all gods children. I learned to ask for help there is no shame in this because I don't have all the answers, and out of weakness came strenght. This supernatural power is a mystery I don't have to figure it out, even though I would like to I just have to accept it. The universe runs itself it doesn't need my help, I get in the flow I allow god to be god I get out of the way I trust the universe to unfold in perfect harmony. My life is part of that. God holds me in the palm of his hand even though many times I have stumbled and fell he gently picks me up he has sent theHolySpirit and the archangels to help me. They give me comfort, wisdom, knowledge, and understanding. Because I had a messed up life I hid in a bottle from my drunkeness came sobriety and the program has delivered me from a self created hell. I am on a spiritual path, so the 12 steps is like that led zeppelin song—a stairway to heaven.

JANUARY-31-2012

Markings in dry clay dissapear only when the clay is soft again. Scars upon the self dissapear only when one becomes soft within. Through out life but especially during youth many scars are inflicted some of them are the results of violence, abuse, rape or humilation and failure, others are caused by misadventure. So unless we recover from these injurys these scars mar us forever. The scriptures urge us to withdraw from our own lusts and sins, but scars that have happened through no fault of our own may also bar us from spiritual success. Unfortunately its often easier to give up a bad habit then the incisions of others violence. The only way is through self cultivation because doctors, priests and sponsors can only do so much. The true cause of healing is up to me alone. To do this I must acguire many methods and travel widely struggle to overcome my personal phobiasAnd most important try not to acguire any new problems because this will bar me from true communion with God. Anyway in my personal life I have struggled with phobias and I do realize the violent crime of being raped as a boy certainly had a shattering effect also the violence inflicted on me mostly from my father and most of this happened before I was 10years old I hadnt even reached my teenage years I had a heavy load. I needed guidance there is no shame in this a child is eager to be shown the way by his parents and so I am wise to recognize that in spiritual terms we are like children and our success will come quicker if we find and follow a wise teacher, I must have a sincere desire to learn and grow. I can gain perspective of God by studying his word. I can look for the larger lessons I gain mastery over fear, doubt, and anxiety I can live in a state of understanding, contentment, and acceptance. So a few things are reguired, the first is I suspend my mistrust of the unkown and allow GOD to lead so I become receptive of his assitance. The second one is that I quiet the demands of my ego because it cant answer my questions about life. So I must realize that going from A to Z is not the way, so i learn to get from A to B then from B to C I learn to travel step by step dealing always with what is immediately at hand and bringing complete focus and concentration to the moment and by doing this I fall into step and receive the creative power of the universe. I let the past and the future go and meet the present with a open mindThe book of changes says the image of Meng is that of a stream beginning to flow down a mountainside filling each ravine and hollow place as it goes so if I persevere in following JC seeking his counsel and filling in the gaps in my character as they are revealed I will be led to a lasting success so I must become childlike because children make the best students. I seek truth in an open and unstructured manner and the secrets of the universe will be revealed.

JANUARY-2012-THE BOOK OF CHANGES

A change in attitude delivers me from difficulties so the higher power uses conflicts and obstacles to teach us lessons-that we refuse to learn in a easier way, but they only darken my doorstep until I have acknowledged the lesson. Anyway as long as I ignore or resist it remains my constant companion, as soon as I accept its presence as a sign that some self correction is needed, my deliverance begins. The only way to dispel trouble and regain peace of mind is to change my attitude. I begin my deliverance by forgiven others I clean the slate and begin new. Next I restore my inner balance, I don't try to force progress. My ego prevents deliverance by holding on too a incorrect attitude. To be truly free of inferior influences I must firmly break with them in my mind, until this inner disengagement is complete no external action will remove them. So by sincerely seeking help from GOD I can root this out and become free. I need a breakthrough so I am not drawn back into bad habits. Because I want this difficulty that has oppresed me for a long time to be dissolved. Anyway in a great storm the wise bird returns to her nest and waits patiently So in times of difficulty I should not be seduced into struggling, striving or seeking solutions through aggressive action. Success is met by waiting modestly for the guidance of the creator. Because trying times are a test to my integrity and commitment to proper principles. At times in my life I have reacted to challenges with fear, anger mistrust and a stubborn desire to strike out and eliminate difficulty once and for all. While the temptation to act in this way can be great to do so can only lead to misfortune, and the loss of hard won ground. The way of the sober mature person faced with difficulty is that of non—action I do not strive for recognition or resolution or try to conquer others. I retreat into my center and cultivate humility, patience on this path of acceptance, self inquiryand self improvement I obtain the aid of the creator and meet with success after the storm has passed. The temptation to act harshly will well up I do not give in so by yielding the matter to the sage I meet with good fortuneI cannot succeed with out the aid of others I seek company and the counsel of those who are sincerely devoted to higher truth. JANUARY-31-2012-Making love is natural so why be ashamed of it? that seems simple but its actually a great challenge because to many layers of meaning have been imposed on sex. Religions straightjacket it, ascetics deny it, romantics glorify it intellectuals theorize about it and obsessives pervert it. These actions have nothing to do with lovemakeing they come from fanaticism and compulsive behavior. Can I actually master the challenge of having lovemakeing be open and healthySo it should not be used as leverage, manipulation selfishness or abuse, and it should not be a ground for compulsions and delusionsSexuality is an honest reflection of our inner most person and we should ensure that its expression is healthy.

51

Richard Kane

FEBUARY 1-2012

Because I am a follower of the way, I seek truth so I understand that a diverse personality is problematic only if some aspects dominate to the exclusion of the others This is unbalance, if there is constant alteration between all aspects then equilibium is possible. Like the planets feelings instincts and emotions must be kept in a constantly rotating order. Then all things have there place and the problems of excess are avoided. Just as the sun is at the center of our solar system, so too must the mind of wisdom be the center our diverse personalitys, if our minds are strong then the various parts of our lives will be held firmly to there proper course and there will be no chance of deviation. I realize that most of my life I tried to deny certain parts fragmentation does not work because I am a whole person so I cant be split. So I was very confused about my sexuality I had extreme guilt and I thought having sexual feelings and thoughts was wrong and evil. I do understand that because of my experience I became a victim of a sex crime I was raped by a man i was 7 I was never treated for this trauma I remained untreated for over 40years, so I developed complexes and phobias. I am still recovering in this area. This is a very important part of my recovery in our book in chapter-5-one of the inventorys is on our sex life we are to pray for the right ideal. God please help me because I don't know what the right ideal is. I have allowed fear to rule my life and I rarely allowed people to get close to me I had that pit in my stomach. I always looked at people and couples they seemed so happy and natural I didn't know how to do that I was so alone and afraid I put on the tough front you know we don't do our dirty laundry in public. I had this stain of being raped and it stayed on me, it was powerful I couldn't drink it away, I tried to ignore it I also tried making believe it never happened—I also tried telling myself that I made it up and that it was a lie—I knew it was true I felt trapped I decided to hide it I became silent I kept this a secret. From this point on shame ruled my life and I acted out on this belief, my actions showed the results of my thinking. I have faced these demons by the power of GOD and I am getting better. I tell you the truth I am tired of carrying this cross and I want it to end, I want this ressurected life because my mind is my problem, I don't need to be restored. I need a whole new mind with a new heart. I am like that guy in the bible called legion, he had so many demons Jesus came and cast them out into a herd of pigs. The pigs ran off a cliff into the water and drowned. Jesus please take my demons and cast them out and drown them I am asking for your help.

FEBUARY-2012-RENEWING OF THE MIND

My mind needs to be renewed daily I must replace old ideas with new ones. Today I must submit my will to God and walk in truth. Because knowledge of the truth will set me free. I am an alcoholic I havent had a drink in over 10years I live one day at a time. The more I let go and surrender old ways of thinking the better I get. This process involves that I become aware of my negative thoughts this can be painful. Because being purified means looking at all my impure thoughts, which will lead to impure actions. So I become more aware of these thoughts because they don't line up withGODS way some of them are criticism, judgeing, gossip, putting others down also prejudice and boasting. All of these come from my ego. There is a path I can follow that will show me a new and better way. I can become useful and a instrument for peace. I must be willing to be used for a higher purpose, I must serve others then my own needs will be met. The great spirit the king of the universe has allowed me to come back into the 12 step recovery movement. So I have come to believe in the power of love, the Bible says God is love is this true—of course it is. How else could I have gotten here. My life has been spared by this power. So will I let God use me for his purpose—or will I try to use GOD for my purpose-The question is who am I living for—do I have what it takes to live my life for God. Can I walk this walk and what are my convictions will I take a stand for them, what have I done with my life has it honored GOD, my slate has been wiped clean by his grace so I can begin and start to live this way.

FEBUARY 1-2012

The realization that God loves us takes away all fear, doubt regret and remorse-shame of the past and dread of the future. Such love transends all understanding it supplys us with infinite patience enduring courage and complete trust in GOD, if we could love God with a fraction of the love he has for us, our eyes would be open to a new vision not only for ourselves but all of mankind. Love provides us with the opportunity to better the world by extending our hand to those in need. By allowing Gods love to radiate through me, I light the way for those who are still living in the darkness of addiction, depression and depair. I have lived in the darkness because iwas raped at 7

I became a victimof that crimeand this caused deep emotional scarsAll the recovery books I read including the big book promises all this joy, and they talk about a joy in living. I wonder to myself how many of them where raped by a man as a boy. Stopping drinking hasn't made this problem any better I needed extra help. I am reading the-I—CHING—the book of changes it says only those who practice innocence, acceptance, and detachment inherit true joy in the world. The I ching teaches us again and again that joy and success cannot be forced or stolen—they are achieved gradually and steadilly by those who relate correctly to others and the higher power. The imageof 2 lakes joined together to keep from drying up, so this is a encouragement to join with like minded people on the same spiritual12 step path, in my heart I must be firm in holding to what is good, honest, and correct. So in my thoughts and actions be gentle and accepting—those who persevere on this path will meet with true joy and lasting success, and those who are sincere in resisting inferior influences meet with good fortune. Those who abandon correctness for temporary pleasures do not. so if I sacrifice principles for a momentary pleasure or gain I will never know true joy because inner conflict ends when we turn our hearts and minds permentaly to what is higher.

FEBUARY-2-2012

In this life sometimes the forces of darkness and disruption show up. When this happens what can I do? I can choose to quietly retreat because to struggle or resist in anger only adds fuel to the fire. A sober person accepts there is a natural ebb and flow between the forces of light and darkness. Wisdom is not gained in resisting, but in responding appropiately. Just as a plant which sprouts in the dead of winter is doomed, and one which sprouts in spring flourishes, and so it is with us. Success and prosperity come to those who advance in times of light—and retreat in times of darkness. I do have a choice so when I calmly accept that the energies at this moment are against me, I can wisely choose to withdraw into the safety of stillness. In this dignified and balanced manner I protect myself from negative influences. When the clamorings of my ego interferes with retreat—this invites humilation. So I devote myself to quiet truthand not too emotional struggle, when one accepts the neccesity of retreat the path becomes easy and clear.—THE PATH—CONstancy in correct thought and action is the order of the day. So rather than letting my head be turned by fantasy, I simply hold steady on my spiritual path. So while the world reforms around you—do not indulge in judgement, impatience or ambitous thinking so by concerning yourself only with what is essential and true. Deal only with what is in front of you and your correct relationship to it—you will meet with good fortune now. Do not expect to much to soon. That which is worthwhile is created slowly and carefully. There is danger of being swayed by external circumstances, so to measure or compare ourselves to others is too depart from the path and invite misfortune. That which is sought in a incorrect fashion is never obtained. Concetrate on my attitude rather than my goals. Do not become restless for constant change allow GOD to work it out in his own way. Because takeing over brings a fall. So here is a way to deal with my shortcomeings—my imperfections and failures are as much a blessing from God as my successes and talents and I lay them both at his feet. So when I fail at something I don't wallow in shame-and I say to myself—I have not sinned against GOD. I have behaved in such a way as to inhibit my union with GOD, and these behaviors are obstacles to my finding a spiritual solution, so beginning right now I will work at removeing these obstactles from my life. So any activity grounded in truth brings progress and good fortune. I make progress like a tree does bending around obstacles rather than confronting them by pushing upwards steadily and gently, there is nothing to be feared from others now. I feel free to ask for help from those who are in a position to give it. As above so it is below. The confidence needed to push upward is found not in my ego but in my relationship with GOD. Success is attined as a result of careful attention to self examination and self improvement, so progress is made in steps not leaps. Disengage ego and ambition do not hurl yourself at a closed door. Because when all barriers to progress are removed, the degree of that success will be determined by the closeness of my alliance with GOD.

FEBUARY-2012 THE MIND OF CHRIST

—Jesus said a new heart I will give you a new heart and a new spirit and I will take away the stoney heart and, You will walk in my statutes and heed my ordinances and do them. The Bible tells us we have the mind of christ and a new heart and spirit. I can make tremendous progress simply by learning how to discern life and death. If I am thinking according to the mind of christ—my thoughts will be positive. So enough can never be said about the

power of being positive. GOD is positive and if I want to flow with him I must get on the same wave length. According to PSALM-3-God is our glory and the lifter of our heads and he wants to lift everything our hopes, attitudes, moods-my head, hands, and heart—my whole life he is our divine lifter. How can I overcome depression? It's a negative thought that presses me down. So being negative wont solve my problem it will only add to them. I can recognize that depression steals life and light. It also opresses a persons spiritual freedom and power the longer it is allowed to remain the harder it becomes to resist. So how can I resist-by remembering the good timesInPSALM-143-I remember the days of old, I meditate on all your doings I ponder the works of yourhands I praise the lord in the midst of the problem—I lift my hands in worship. I spread forth my hands to my soul thirsts after you like a thirsty land. God alone can water a thirsty soul, don't be decieved into thinking that anything else can satify you fully and completely so chaseing after the wrong will always leave you dissapointed. And this opens the door for depression and a whole lot more. I can ask GOD for help like in psalm-143 answer me speedily O Lord for my spirit hide not your face from me lest I become like those who go down into the pit. I am simply saying—hurry up GOD because I am not going to be able to hold on much longer without you. I learn to listen for the Lord—so I can hear your loveing and kindness in the morning For only on you do I lean and in you do I trust, cause me to know the way where I should walk as I lift up my inner self to you. I pray for deliverance-deliver me JC from my enemies, I flee to you to hide me. I must keep my mind on GOD and not the problem. I seek GODS wisdom, knowledge and leadership—teach me to do your will for you are my GOD-let your good spirit lead into a level country and into the land of uprightness. MARCH-2012The door of hope is open to all victims by recognizing and resolving all the pain because of my past I decided as a child to put on a mask and to cover up the intensity of my abuse. I realize that the sex abuse has taken a toll on my life. Of course it has what else could happen I mean to say I was very young I hadnt even developed into a teenager iwas a child this caused much anguish. I was confused angy disgraced and full of shame. I kept it all locked up deep inside I thought this was the answer I became a prisoner because I refused to talk about it. This was a deep wound time doesn't heal these kind of wounds. I never developed a healthy identity and this violent crime just added to that. Because I was use to being abused I developed a cold hard heart I had to survive because violence was normal to me and the family never talked about anyof this. I survived long enough so I can get the help I needed silence about all this didn't help. As they say in the bible I kept going around the same mountain denial kept me going around and around I prentended every thing was alright. I knew I was wounded and shattered I didn't know I could be put back together I could be a whole person. I hid all my feelings this is very painful. Alcohol became my savior I could be numb and free as long as I stayed drunk—I had my secrets no one must ever know I was raped I felt enormous shame and iwas stained and dirty I felt perverted I felt like I caused it I knew all about betrayal. IS there a solution getting drunk seemed like the answer and in a strange way it did become my answer because of my alcoholism I have come to know a spiritual way of life. THrough the 12 steps I am reborn and becoming a child of God—and he doesn't see me like the abuse survivor he created me and god is love—anyway for a while iwas mad at GOD because he was there when I got raped and he didn't stop it. Although I understand now that he stopped that man from killing me he certainly could have done that I was powerless. GOD I thank you for saveing my life so I pray father I don't understand what is happening and what you are asking me to do is beyond my abilityand my body feels the pain my mind is in a state of confusion I feel a deep sense of despair I am being consumed by fears insecuritys and shame. However I freely choose to allow the holy spirit to persuade me and I cry out holy spirit help my unbelief. I choose to obey GOD and his word and with faith I receive my miracle and my blessings right now amen

MARCH-17-2012

I want to be a power of example, so I must continue to stay sober. Can I become a walking example of the big book. This is a worthy goal and there is a 12 step answer to every problem. Alcohol is the sympton I am the problem, God is the solution—I am a piece of GOD, when I accepted JC into my life I found new power and peace—I heard him knock I opened the door to my heart. At times I try to shut him out because I am acting in shameful ways and I don't want him to know. Anyway he knows and he is there with me even in the darkness because he cares he sends the holy spirit to guide and comfort me. When my pride and arrogance get in the way I refuse to listen and when my sanity returns I begin again and I listen. I am learning to follow the guidance and do what I am supposed to do. Staying sober is my gift to GOD and I must stay on this path—I have room for improvement the 10step helps me to work on that. Oh I still stumble not from booze from the speed bumps of life and when my self will runs riot I create chaos. When I get back on the path I soon realize this life is a blessing and I am glad to have it. I can make a difference I can do something good and make the universe a better place by changing one person me. I can choose peace, love, and harmony. We are all one and we come from the same creative force. I can get in the flow and allow it to take me and do what it wants with me. When I let go and allow I am in the flow I let it be this is great and awesome the power of love flows everywhere.

MARCH-2012

I continue in my journey, this road is long and difficult. My ego is the problem when it becomes inflated I act out in selfish inmature ways. I forget I am a child of God fear takes over and runs the show false pride and arrogance come back I am going around the same old mountain. I have done this for to longi am getting tired and I want to move forward. I am going to be55 in June what have I lived my life for-I lived in delusionville thinking these pursuits of pleasure would make me happy and I have traveled many roads to nowhere. All of this leftme empty alone and angry. My mind gets cluttered with the past—so much time is waisted with these memories that cant be changed. The pain from childhood still lingers—and it seems like yesterday they are very old they still have power. Doyou know what it feels like to be raped? IWAS 7 and it was a man a stranger I didn't fully understand it. I was very afraid I remained silent—iwanted to tell my father what that man did, however I chose not to because. I feared my father and his anger I was convinced he would kill me he said them words to me and he was capable of that. I do have scars most of them are not visible will I ever overcome these thoughts—going to 12 step meeting s for my drinking hasn't helped in this area—how could it most people cant identify with these incidents most people were not beating and raped is this self pity I don't think it is. I am human I get self pity it passes with time I am free and I don't have to pour booze down my throat to hide my sorrows. I have made peace with my past Alcohol Is the symptom I am the problem I still act out in other ways these habits can be changed I really want to be rid of them and one day I will, progress has been made I am on the right road sometimes I wonder if I have made any progress because I still stumble over the same stones one day I will learn to walk around them.

MARCH-31-2012

The I Ching teaches that all conflict is in the end is a inner conflict, so when I see it beginning I am obliged not to pursue it. Why because this only compounds my misfortune. So the only way to live free of conflict is to hold steadily to proper principles. Through balance, patience, and devotion to inner truth I will rise above every challenge, so the proper response to conflict is disengagement. Do not fight with others for center stage, because that which is truly valuable is gained through quiet perseverance, modesty, and a sincere devotion to GOD. All true progress is made on the path to correctness. Lasting progress is won through quiet discipline. Heaven can exist on earth, for those who maintain correct thoughts and actions.

APRIL-25-2012

Foolish leaders indulge themselves, leaving there fields untilled and there storehouses empty. they wear impressive clothes, brandish sharp words and weapons are addicted to food, drink, and possesions—this is the road to excess not the way of the TAO. Following taosist principles the samurai lived simply and delibrerately. Believing that excess weakened the spirit they did not clutter there lives with many possesions, they didn't waste anything they practiced economy not out of financial need, because they knew that discipline in small things builds strenght of character. I can benefit from the example of the samurai. So when I am feeling confusion. conflict, also addiction and feelings of powerlessness-all these come from excessive self indulgence-this dissipates my vital energy. When I lose my center it undermines my strenght. so like the samurai tao leaders maintain power by removing clutter this creates more space I give myself room to breath, The 10th step is a tool that helps me keep my ego in check its very similar to the practice of the samurai so when self seeking becomes excessive I am out of balance and my behavior will show that. So I must get back to being centered—the simple truth is every moment contains the teaching that I need at that time. It is not always immediately apparent why a thing is happening because the sage is often inclined to work in a roundabout fashion—nonetheless whatever is happening now is what must happen. My only task is to trust the process and allow the lesson to seep in. So when I am resisting and preventing progress—success is still possible because every opposistion carries within it the seeds of agreement, cease resisting yourself and others—let go of dark thoughts and agrresive actions. By returning to acceptance neutrality and devotion to the ways of GOD. I dissolve the opposition within and open the way for understanding and good fortune, mistrust of fate leaves me isolated and alone—buy rejoining the path I return to joy I stay on the 12 step path back to life I return to love.

MAY-6-2012

I can have a dream and it can come true my dream is a book contract with a big publisher and a contract with a agent I will then see my book in bookstores I will have success iwill go to a book signing I can also have a family a wife and kids a nice small home and a great job this is my dream andGOD, JC. and the holy spirit can provide all of this, nothing is impossible forGOD.

.JUNE-5-2012

The real me is not my body or my mind I am a divine being having a temporary human physical experience, I am a channel for the great spirit of the universe I am at peace with this journey forgiveness is very vital and I have forgiven all my abusers I realize they didn't know what they were doing they were insane. I thought iwasted a lot of time what is time is it really wasted all experiences are lessons and the dark side teaches me about my weaknesses. I learned I must develop my strenghts and manage my weaknesses and if I am manifesting undesirable conditions I change my ideas and viewpoint about them and a new set of conditions will appear. Today I turned 55 that is a fact and I am happy to be sober 11years and I am in very good shape my mind is healing all my so called issues exist only in my mind I must be renewed daily I am new creation in Christ.

Friday, JUNE 15

I went and had a reading with a medium at the journey within it's a siritual church and this was a new experince. This is what went down I closed my eyes and picked 6stones and six cards, she began to tell me about a presence of a man who said he was very sorry for much of the past he said he couldn't express his love for me because he had to many of his own wounds. He said he is proud of me for being sober and he attends AA meetings with me in spirit. This is something very new and there is much to think about I am still learning. It lasted about 40 minutes I don't know if I will have another one, I do feel more at peace with my father and the past. He was a flawed human being like me—she did say he is not in hell I am grateful he isnt and that he is learning the lessons there that he didn't learn down here. he said I have courage to write my life story and to deal with my sex abuse, I do have a better understanding of my father I have a better relationship with him now than I did when he was alive, I am open to learn more and I continue to go to the journey within.

JUNE-30-2012

Life is a struggle and suffering is part of it. Pain comes to all whether we want it or not so when I act out I then stumble and fall doubts creeps back in and I feel guilty because I did it again, shame seems to be my constant companion, my past keeps comeing back to haunt me. JUSt when I think I made a breakthrough and I am over this stuff I have a breakdown shame returns did it ever really leave no its inside of me, because I believe its so—is it true—do I feel dirty inside because of the sex abuse and being raped or is it some excuze—I am not sure. Who am I anyway—I don't know so that makes me who I am. I am a complete human being, I just feel incomplete, I judge my life by these standards this American dream and the standards of being a man. I feel very incompleteI have not achieved the all american standards—mom, baseball apple pie white picket fence a dog a wife and kids I have none of these am I any less a man than them that have these. Am I a human being and are we all one created by the same source. Why all this hatred and wars, we have gangs it's the same cycle of violence and revenge I been part of that it solves nothing when I hurt another human being I am hurting my self. What the world needs is love not hatred and violence and rape, prositutes street life gangs drugs and booze it's the road to destruction. We can make a difference with love as our guide build a new world with peace harmony and oneness open our minds toheal all people and diseases is this a ideal, can this impossible dream become possible-THeBIBLE SAYS WITH GOD all things are possible and I believe in the power of love and we can all do our part and make this into reality.

JULY-2012

IS rape a crime is being raped as a boy any different then it is for a girl. Did I become a victim when iwas raped, I was 7 it was a man I couldn't make him stop I was totally powerless. Our first step talks about powerlessness over alcohol there are many forms of being powerless ask a young child who gets constant violent beatings lets not talk about such things these things arent nice they shatter the illusion of the perfect American family. My struggles in life continue I am 55 sober 11years these incidents happened a long time ago they seem to stick around there is a cycle to life because of some of the events I have questions the answers don't exist the people I would ask why are not here they are dead so I will never know. I wonder how that man felt when he raped me did he feel powerful he must have realized he was hurting me—did he care was he selfish or was he sick was he another grown up victim who became a perpetrator. I heard it said at meetings hurt people hurt others because of my age I was a easy target so be it. I will say this I was abused sexualy more than once all of them were men and iwas under 10 I really wish they never happened. When I became a teenager it created to many questions—I also had doubts and fear. I did not feel special these incidents created a dirty, filthy, perverted self hatred I wanted to annihilate myself my strong emotions lead to many violent encounters my path in life became dark when iwas raped and also when iwas beaten down by my father. I did what any victim does i did nothing I took it all. Until one day I lashed out in rage i fought back against people who had nothing to do with my abuse it was the wrong choice fear ruled my life, BECAUSE OF MY BOOZING I ENDED UP IN 12 STEP MEETINGS I recovered from alcoholism of course alcohol is only the symptom—this other stuff isnt so simple. Because the road ahead is dark I trip over many speed bumps where is the light my past seems to *hold me back or maybe it pushes me forward I don't know. I haveconfronted some of the demons from my past—life is such a struggle back and forth I go—I run toGOD please help me—sometimes in shame I try to run away fromGod—he sends his angels to protect and guide me although at the time I say I don't want it—I am always grateful later on that GOD doesn't always listen to me.*

JULY-2012

Jimi Hendrix sings with the power of love anything is possible yes this is true the bible saysGod is love and the source of all power we are all one—we are the world. The Beatles said all you need is love. Life is a journey and it can get heavy my life was blown apart many moons agoJesus came for the brokenhearted I am still alive and I don't why i remain sober free from alcohol—yet I am still bound to my past. Memories race into my mind I don't want them—what I resist persists this zen saying seems true to me, can I make these memories go away they seem to have power what can I do—I calmly realize and become aware these thoughts are old memories and they are gone I come to the present moment I also remember by christs blood I am set free he paid for it all. I get weary my soul is heavy I am tired of this stuff in my mind, I ask JC to take it—so why does it come back again and again, did he not hear me, where is he when I need him I gotta rest. PEACE and GOD are one I am part ofGOD.

JULY-15-2012

I am doing alright I am grateful I am going to this spiritual church called the journey within I like it helps me maintain my sobriety and some balance, they have mediums there they contact the other sideanyway every week on Sunday I go there for a few months they sing this song where I sit is holy, holy is the ground forest mountain river listen to the sound great spirit circles all around me—who I am is holy holy are we—body thought emotion connecting you and me great spirit circles all around me—what I do is holy—holy is my way work and play together celebrate the day great spirit circles all around me this is really a great song puts me in contact with spirit of the universe I seek peace the truth sets me free, I want to help the world have peace we are all one. planet earth is a great circle because of 12 step recovery I am open minded GOD is love and so areall of us we are the world and the human family is all connected lets end violence and work towards a better earth we all can help achieve this.

JULY-2012

I am learning tocultivate my own garden, can I be both martial and spiritual. To be martial requires discipline, courage, and perseverance-and it has nothing to do with killing. People fail to look beyond this narrow aspect of the warrior so they overlook all the other qualities that are gained from training. A warrior is not a cruel murderer, he is a protector of ideals, principles, and honor-also noble and heroic, the warriors main opponent is within, because within his personality are a wide array of demons to be conquered. fear, laziness, ignorance, also selfishness, ego and many more. To actualy over come ones defects is the true nature of victory.

JULY-20-2012

Be glad today how very easily is hell undone. Ineed but tell myselfi am the holy son of God, I cannot suffer or be in pain so I let this thought change me. A miracle has lighted up all darkness for time has lost its hold on me. The son of God has come in glory to redeem the lost to save the helpless and to give to the world the gift of his forgiveness-Gods son has come to set us free. I was meditating the other day I got directions to read page 36-from the book Gods promises for men-so here it is—the sun shall no longer be your light by day nor for happiness shall the moon give light to you but theLORD to you will be a everlasting light, and your Godyour glory-your sun shall no longer go down nor shall your moon withdraw itself, for theLord will be your everlasting light and the days of your mourning shall be ended. This is awesome I have been praying for years forGod to restore the years the locust ate, that's almost50years-God is my best friend he justifies me he washed me clean and I am a new creation.

JULY-2012

Saint francis says its better to understand than to be understood. My journey took me to a medium where I had a reading—she got in touch with my father he is dead since 1979-I now understand and I realize my father was a impefect human being who made some mistakes some of them impacted me. life at times seems so incomplete and there are struggles, I been layed off again that's the way it is in construction—so I didn't take it personal thats growth, my ego wants me to think I did something wrong or I got screwed anyway I have been working for Wetlands for a while and they always called me back after a layoff, so I am alright. My ego is the main problem it doesn't want me to feel contented—it wants me uneasy, uptight, afraid full of questions and ideals of how it should be. these ideals of perfection are a big setup for failure because life is impefect and the universe is full of mystery. So what life seems to go on with out my imput, my heart beats with out my permission the sun shines and the moon and the stars are in the sky, I didn't put them there. Energy is everywhere I am from that same energy do I think the creator made a mistake, yes sometimes I do because of my past and all them abuses, I must let GOD make something good out of that mess, so it becomes a message. There is hope, love, peace and understanding, joy and also there is hard times pain struggle, questions and uncertainity its all part of the path on this journey and I accept all of it.

JULY-29-2012

I have been training since the winter with boxing. I have done up to 13-3 minute rounds with a 30second rest on the heavy bag, I have sparred 10minutes with someone, I also have been running almost every day I run2 miles on the weekday then on Sunday I run 5 miles. I lost about 30pounds since the winter I feel good I am healing in body, mind and spirit. I am now working towards 12 years of sobriety this is importantbecause I did stop for over 12 years I went back to the bottle—I learned from this experience—so what did I learn alcohol is the sympton I am the problem ialso got a sponsor read the big book and took inventory did the step work I didn't do these things before anyway times goes very quickly I am55-I don't let my feelings run my life. God is in charge of my life—he knows I need a lot of help, so he sent the holy spirit as my guide. my sanity is restored I am not afraid of alcohol because of step 10 I have power in my life step11 says with prayer and meditation all things are possible. I am not afraid of life or failure because the holy spirit turns these trials into lessons. I am still on this journey of growing up. I have a God consciouness I must try to be like jesus, this is a tall order and I havent achieved that I know I am on the right track.

AUGUST-6-2012

I read the bible and I really like psalm 103-because it says he heals all my diseases and forgives all my sins. This is really awesome because I committed many crimes and I wasn't always drunk when I did them. I am not that person now because I have allowed GOD and the 12 steps to transform me into a useful worthwhile human being. I still have my faults I am a flawed human human being i am a lot like my parents and I forgive them they are flawed to we are all GODs children. I realizeI am responsible for my own life, because I turned my life over to jesus I am reborn a new creation—oh I still have many of my old ways I am on the right path GOD has all answers—I must learn to wait patiently on the Lord, his plan works much better than mine.

AUGUST-10-2012-THE POWER OF INTENTION

The universe is pure power and all loveing. so when I tap into this infinite source I am acting just like it. This is my goal to be like my source so when I want love—imust be loveing, when I want friends I must be friendly. my ego creates all the problems and drama in my life. The ego wants to be separate it wants me to feel like I don't fit in that I am better than some and worse than others, it also doesn't want me asking for help it thinks that is a sign of *weakness. Of course we know that asking for help is a strenght in all the 12 step groups I am involved with we help each other. I am dependent on God and people, I don't live on this earth alone, we all have the same needs and we are all one people we are Gods children. Its my wants that cause my problems, the ego is selfish- The spirit of the universe is unselfish and loveing. I must learn to let go of old ideas, there are so many of them so many of them came from my family—I learned mistrust and fear I acted out on these misbeliefs, I thought I should be able to handle my own life don't ask for help and do everything myself, we know the results of this kind of thinking. I bottomed out and iwas brought to my knees. This is when life turned around because I surrendered and let the spirit of the universe run my life all good comes from God, peace and harmony came into my life I stopped fighting I let go and I let god I must practice letting go daily because my ego wants me to get identity from the things I think are mine my pickup truck or my motorcycle also my being in the laborers union I think I am finding myself in these things I never quite make it and end up losing myself in them this is the fate of the ego. How do turn this around GOD is the answer he handles all my life I have to give it to him he wont force himself on me I have free will I still sometimes take it back I get fed up with myself and I surrender to GOD this path is a lot of back and forth I will continue to try and grow into the person God wants me to be its being more like CHRist it's a tall order I am on the right track.*

SEPTEMBER-2-2012

When does it end, when does the anguish stop. No one was there to stop that man from rapeing me—I was powerless to stop him. I have not fully achieved freedom from these thoughts—iwas a defenseless boy-We talk about being powerless over alcohol, there are many forms off powerlessness so what hurts more getting raped or my drinking. I have power to stop drinking—I had no power to stop from being raped. What good can come from this, this memorie has stayed with me for over forty years. What do I do, where do I go how can I overcome this—I have to face this powerful demon. I only hope it doesn't follow me when I leave this earth. I don't want to remember this in Heaven. Just recently because of the news about the men that where sexualy abused at Penn state I prayed for all the people involved and I hope they seek help for there pain, I really hope they start recovery a lot sooner than I did—iwaited over 40years I caused so much anguish, fear did that. I learned the hard way these wounds don't go away and my life has been affected because of these events. I realize I need God, Jesus, and the holy spirit to heal my mind and emotions because I haven't been able to just shake it off, however I know I am on the right path. I have sought extra help and even though the journey has been very painful I also have peace, so I will not give up I will continue to go forward. I need guidance because the damage caused by sex abuse to a young boy is very severe. I do know God is the answer, and he will help me reclaim my life and become healthy, whole, and happy.

SEPTEMBER-PRAYER

DIVine heath is mine in JESUS name I declare and receive divine love, and perfect health. I speak life, abundance, prosperity, peace, love-harmony. Sobriety is more than not drinking, when I make my will conform with his then I am using it correctly. GOD wants to bless me-I gotta get out of the way. The ego is the problem, love is the answer because God is love-forgiveness heals all wounds.

SEPTEMBER-2012

HERe is a American indian prayer-grandfather look at our brokenness we know that in all of creation only the human family has strayed from the sacred way we are the ones who are divided and we are the ones who must come back together to walk in the sacred way-grandfather sacred one teach us love, compassion, honor so that we may heal the earth and heal each other. This is a awesome prayer, I have come to realize that I can help heal the earth by doing my part and changing one person, because every thought and action I take effects the whole world. I can help people come out of the darkness by being a bright light because the love light is within all of us. A new earth is possible all countrys and all people are one we are the human family we can help each to awaken there is plenty for all of us lets help each to fufill a divine purpose, we can achieve peace and togetherness. Because separation doesn't work and my *vision is a end to all gang violence, wars oppression and torture we can all do our part, I can be the change I want this or something better for all people.*

SEPTEMBER-2012

Invisibility is the best advantage, but if forced to a confrontation come out with all your skill. There once was a roadside vendor who sold fruit to passer bys. He was a cheery old man, one day a young bully began to harass him. The old man tried very hard to avoid the confrontation, the bully became convinced he had a coward to mess with. When the moment of attack came, the old man defeated him with superior boxing skills. After that the old man was never seen again. Because he had shown his superiority at a critical moment, but once he had exposed himself he disappeared. In this competive world it is best not to show off or make flamboyant gestures, because this will only attract the hostility of others. The wise accomplish all they want with out arousing the envy or scorn of others They don't bring attention to themselves I am learning new ways of doing things this is wisdom.

SEPTEMBER-2012

Jimi Hendrix sang with the power of love anything is possible, is this true—oh yes it is because ofGods great love for me, and the 12step recovery programs I participate in. I have been transformed from the inside out-this is a message of love. All addictions are fear based behaviors, my life was out of control. I had no power to stop, my will was useless force didn't work also fear of going to jail or any of that kind of stuff didn't work either. Power is the answer, the great spirit of the universe came to my aid when I surrendered. I have power now and I use it in a correct manner. If the 3 letter word, God offends me I just add another o to it, then it says good do good don't do bad sounds like spiritual wisdom to me, simple wisdom andsimple truth they both set me free. I am free to be a human being who is growing with understanding, love and compassion. I am being helpful and not hurting others or myself this is a spiritual path I do intend to stay on this path the rest of my life.

SEPTEMBER-12-2012

There are times when I am still attached to my past, my personal history keeps me from being in the now. The point is that because of my past I am dancing to a tune thrown at me by others. In order for me to step up onthis path to my sacrced quest I must toss out the idea that I am unable to bee free from the past. I can learn to eraze my personal history, than I will be free. How can this be true in a moment of satori or instant awakeing I can drop my personal history, just like that I can drop it right now. Thats it if I don't have a story, then I don't have to live up to that. I can turn the page and write a new story. To be born again is to let the past go and look without condemnation upon the present, I am being asked to let the future go, and place it inGods hands. I will see by this experience that I have laid the past and the present in his hands too. The past can no longer punish me. Because I have a limitless source of inner power I can start again with a blank page. Because of my relationship with the highest power all things become possible. There is no limitations the highest good can be achieved—this a divine universe I can find the answer to who am i—since I am not my past, I am a soul with a body—not a body with a soul. A simple life is a sanctified life.

SEPTEMBER-11-2012-ACCEPTANCE

What is my life about what am I living for—will I allow the spirit of the universe to transform me. when I am transformed I can be used for a higher purpose. Anyway despite all my brokenness, pain and failures-God sees something in me and he wants the best for me. The spirit of the universe is all powerful this power is used for the ultimate good. We are all Gods children, many of us where lost I know iwas, he found me in my mess. he cleaned me so I can carry the message of sobriety, hope and recovery, I am human and I will fall short—this doesn't surprize God. i must continue to go forward on this life journey. There is eternity that' means forever a very strange concept for me to understand. This life is short I am 55-it seems like yesterday that iwas 15 a teenager I am grateful I have matured and I don't miss the old life. I realize all that happened needed to happen—because I am exactly where I need to be in this moment. I have all that ineed. My ego is the problem and awareness of that smashes the ego, the ego is all about the past I must stay present peace is here and now so is love I accept all of my life as being perfect.

SEPTEMBER-14-2012

Harry Chapin sang when you comeing dad I don't know when-Let me tell you when my dad came home drunk nothing good ever happened and he never came home sober I don't recall many good memories with my father we never talked or hung out. The trust was broken by the violence and iwas very afraid of him. I didn't feel he loved me—I wanted his love. I accept those where my feelings no one caused them, as a boy I didn't realize I had choices I felt trapped., I learned how to survive. I learned to shut down all my feelings, and pretend everything was alright. I wanted control of course I had no control. Things were controlling me. The past owned me—the abuses and fear ruled my life I felt so alone and helpless. Where was God when I needed him, he must have been sleeping when I got raped this was acruel thing. I managed to survive so I thought—did I really survive—or was God there all along. He did for me what I couldn't he got me through that trial and the pain. God has set me free the rape and the abuse don't own me, I am much more then all of them things
, I am much more than my alcoholism. I am a child ofGod a divine being of light I am full of love, forgiveness and compassion.

SEPTEMBER-18-2012

I ask youGod, to remove my hard heart, because I have need for intimacy. It has to begin with you. God you are my best friend, I ask you to remove my suicidal thoughts, its not a healthy option. I have tried to get my need for intimacy met in some unhealthy ways. By going to prositutes and pornography both of these leave me empty, angry, dirty and feeling full of shame, after all I went through im abuseing myself worse than the people who orignaly abused me I am asking inJESUS name for freedom from this thinking. Richard Kane believedGod and it was reckoned to him as righteousness and Richard was called the friend of God. Well friend I am comeing in great need to heal this broken part of me my wounded soul I am tired of carrying my wounds from childhood my hostility towards others, my feeling alone and unworthy and envy-Oh I am sober and grateful—the pain from my abuses is more real because I am sober I cant run back to my comforter I come to you I do have moments of peace and contentment—I also have times of doubt anguish and darkness. I do know what to do I come to you with fulltrust because I know you are the healer help me realize this truth, I have no doubt in your power to heal my mind and emotions help me stay out of the way. Imust pray and wait.

SEPTEMBER-2012

I have been going to this spiritual church called the journey within. They have mediums, what that means is they communicate with the dead. I started going around 6 months ago I wanted to hear from my father because I have questions about our relationship. He died from his drinking he was 56it was in 1979. I had a messed up relationship with him he inflicted a lot of pain with his violence and he was also very strict. He always drank whiskey I never seen him sober—I always wondered if he remembered any of the beatings we never really talked I never got close with my father a unhealed wound anyway I wondered if he even remembered beating the hedge clippers on top of my head maybe he was in a blackout, he never said he was sorry or apologized for anything. Last Sunday I got a hit at the service from the medium she talked to me and said a man had something to say he apologized for being so strict I told her he was my father. I never heard these words when he was alive I have waited over 45 years to hear them words. I am glad he is alright and learning his lessons in the spiritual realm.

OCTOBER-22-2012-FEAR FROM THE ABUSE

I often ask myself, why did I never get romantic and want to get married. I only dated 4 ladys I am 55 and I haven't dated anyone in over 4 years. I believe in my heart this path is not for me because of the abuse from my childhood and the biggest factor was the rape by a man I was only 7 iwas shattered broken hurt I never learned how to jump over these obstactles. When I became a teenager I was attracted to some girls, I was to afraid to let them know that. I use to think other people could see inside of me, and they knew iwas this dirty filthy useless perverted rape victim. I was very ashamed you know I thought iwas a coward because I didn't fight this man. I knew iwas only 7 when I got older I started boxing I took pride in being able to fight and defend myself I was hideing from the false believe that iwas a coward I began to hide in a bottle of booze so many times through the years I wished that man had killed me. The pain got harder after I stopped drinking my crutch was gone what was I going to do I was sick I wanted my freedom from this pain I had to find a meeting for sex abuse it's a tough issue and its back and forth and we don't give out coins like other 12 step meetings for length of sobriety my healing has to come from GOD I cant measure my progress like my drinking I haven't had a drink in over 11 years yet this pain has followed me most of my life I get ashamed to talk about it at the 12 step meetings I think I sound like a broken record Jesus Christ is the one I need to heal my brokenness he can finish the job and make me whole that is my hope today I bless the whole world with peace love and harmony

OCTOBER-2012

I do not need to pretend that I am anyone other than myself, and I do not need to feel insecure about my perceptions. The self cultivation that I undertake is to perfect who I am not to become someone other than who I am.—I pursue the spiritual path because it gives me satisifaction. Life has its sad and happy moments, I accept them all, there is also times of confusion and serenity these are the moments I seek. I continue to travel this path I do not compare myself to others—let them have there lives, and I will enjoy mine.

OCTOBER-24-2012

Jesus called me and told me to lie down in green pastures of peace and learn to unwind. I get wired out upset and uptight—so why should I feel guilty about resting. This is a very basic human need, JC said I have called you to walk with me down this path of peace. I want you to blaze a trail for others who desire to live in my peaceful presence. I have chosen you not because of your strengths but more for your weaknesses which amplify your need for me. I depend onChrist more and more because he will shower me with peace on this journey.

OCTOBER-25-2012

What is time is it a concept why do we think its so important—does age always bring wisdom. Then why do we hear people say there is no fool like a old fool. Stubborn pride leads to many falls, we all fall big and small—when I get up I must look for the lesson. Life is full of lessons some of them I learned the slow hard way. I have repeated many foolish acts in the 55 years I walked this earth its way to easy to blame booze but what do I say when I act out and im not drunk. I must realize I am the problem. There is a path I must follow to have a good life I am on this sacred quest, because I want to help make the world a better place. I pray and meditate for world peace, I pray for all people and our planet. I pray for peace love and harmony, we are all one—I can help bring change to our planet. I can stand for peace I would like to see a end to all wars, we need to love ourselves and the whole planet. Respect all animals, plants, trees and the water and also each other. WE can do this its, not impossible. We are one because God is one and we are all created by the one creator. Do you remember the song imagine byJohnLennon—imagine all the people living life in peace. wouldnt that be great. What can I do to help that. I can recognize all people are my brothers and sisters, I can be helpful, loving, gentle and kind. I can support peaceful resolution to all conflict.

OCTOBER-26-2012

Discernment means following what inspires me and releasing what diminishes me. Because I am going in a new direction I must learn to be kind to myself, as I practice the wisdom of discernment. I can find my calling in life by listening to my heart, because its my inner compass—I can learn to detach from this noisy world, and follow the deep values in my heart. So I must learn to deal with the challenges. I cannot give in to learned helplessness. My biggest challenge is getting raped at age 7-I thought I would just forget about it and with time it would go away talk about learned helplessness. Well after 40years of pretending I now know better and I have begun to take action for my emotional healing. I must continue this journey on a daily basis, this invisible wound doesn't heal like a broken bone. I have felt overwhelmed and doubted myself on this journey through the darkness of sex abuse—rape is a brutal word that's is what happened why pretend. Anyway I am not my rape, my abuse or my alcoholism I am much more than that. I am a spiritual being. I have allowed these things to diminish mefor to long. I have learned to take a stand and say what can I do about this. I must then follow a course of action. The emotional healing is my greatest need, the past cannot be changed despite this I can grow. I have learned many lessons from this incident. I learned how to forgive myself for not doing nothing for over 40years and the person who did itI have to keep going forward

I continue to share my journey I remained silent for to long—I will not be silenced now. I am not a helpless victim I am not ashamed of who I am, I have the power of GOD living inside of me. He is my best friend, my strength and guide. God knows what I need and he provides it. This moment is all I have my emotional and spiritual needs are greater than my physical needs God is pure love and because I am his child he takes care of me Gods love is in every aspect of me.

NOVEMBER-4-2012

Hurricane Sandy has come and gone leaving behind much wreckage and damage. We are now rebuilding. i lost the power in my house for 5 days I am alright I am a survivor. I used this time to practice more meditation I pray everyday. I am healing body, mind, and spiritI get up early I run 2 miles I do 500pushups in 1 hour then I box 8 rounds on the heavy bag that takes care of my physical needs. I heal my spirit with prayer and meditaion—I also read a lot of spiritual books and I read the 12 step recovery bible. I like to go for a walk by the Hackensack river, I go the the newbridge this is a sacred peaceful place I like to look at the water I make peace and I find tranquility here, sometimes I see rainbows. I try to be a positive person because of the hurricane there is a lot of fear and chaos. I carry a message of love and hope—because God is love and we are all one family the human family we are all his children lets work together for the greatest good I can help out and do my part. There was a lot of damage from hurricane sandy the Jersey shore got hammered and some people got killed I continue to pray and help out anyway I can do something even when I donate one box ofmacroni to the food bank I think of others needs we all need help once in a while there is no shame in that. This journey continues thanksgiveing is comeing up I count my blessings I am sober I have great health a place to live and fellowship and friends, God is my best friend and I am his.

NOVEMBER-2012

I practiced contacting the spirit, I did that exercise out of ritas book.-comminicating with spirits. I seen blue lights and I got a message from a man he called me Richard he said how sorry he was for not being there also the violence he apologized said he is learning his lessons. I asked for guidance from the guide he said that because of all the abuse mostly the rape that I still act out—I am on the right path he said I need to learn to let go and believe. He said I am going to meet a beautiful women, who has children and I will be a great father. The spirits encouraged me to keep going forward—he also told me about the man who raped me when I was 7i wasn't the only one. He was very sick and it happened to him as a boy he is very sorry he realizes the devasting effects it had on my life and the others. He is learning his lessons. The spirit said to stop with the escorts it only diminishes me and thembecause many of them where also abuse victims when I hurt myself I hurt others everything effects the whole I must learn to grow and walk in the spirit, I can let go of this broken behavior.

NOVEMBER-2012

This journey must go on I face my dark side I grow in the light, I am not afraid most of the time, I still get nightmares they have no power to hurt me. GOD is in charge and he is my best friend I hang on I carry on, hope keeps me moveing forward, I am going to start my new book the Bronx street kid this journey must go on we are all important and we serve a higher purpose I pray for world peace. I believe in miracles, staying sober is a gift I cherish this gift. This book is now done I plan on writing my 4th book I will take a break it took over 1 year to write this book I really hope my book helps others—I am thinking of calling my next book—the Bronx street kid this journey goes on thanks everybody for all the support I bless all with peace love and harmony and also abundance of health happiness and good fortune